our *sweet basil*
K I T C H E N

our
sweet basil
KITCHEN

FRESH TWISTS ON FAMILY FAVORITES WITH
RECIPE MASHUPS AND UNIQUE FLAVOR COMBINATIONS

CADE AND CARRIAN CHENEY

SHADOW
MOUNTAIN

This book is for our incredibly wonderful,
sweet, and always hungry children.
We cannot imagine anything better than our
time spent in the kitchen with you.

Design © Shadow Mountain
Art direction by Richard Erickson
Book design by Sheryl Dickert Smith
Production design by Kayla Hackett
Photographs on pages ii, vii, viii, and 174 by Lori Romney.
Cover photographs and all other photographs provided by the authors.
Kitchen by CNJ Cabinets.

Text and photographs © 2017 Sweet Basil Blog LLC

Visit us at ShadowMountain.com

Library of Congress Cataloging-in-Publication Data
Names: Cheney, Cade, author. | Cheney, Carrian, author.
Title: Our sweet basil kitchen : fresh twists on family favorites with recipe mashups and unique flavor combinations / Cade and Carrian Cheney.
Description: Salt Lake City, Utah : Shadow Mountain, [2017] | Includes index.
Identifiers: LCCN 2016033684 | ISBN 9781629722900 (hardbound : alk. paper)
Subjects: LCSH: Cooking, American. | LCGFT: Cookbooks.
Classification: LCC TX715 .C2155 2017 | DDC 641.5973—dc23 LC record available at https://lccn.loc.gov/2016033684

Printed in China
RR Donnelley, Shenzhen, China

10 9 8 7 6 5 4 3 2 1

contents

SIDE DISHES

MAIN DISHES

DESSERTS

introduction

When Carrian was a little girl, her mother would take the family berry picking, and countless, exhausting hours were spent weeding the garden so they could enjoy a bountiful harvest at the end of summer. The fresh foods of the Pacific Northwest, a farm-to-table mentality, and a love for homemade meals were a way of life. Carrian often says that she had no idea just how good she had it. She fell in love with the sweet marionberries from the farm down the road, and she often dipped big, juicy strawberries in the sugar bowl. Her philosophy is "There's nothing like fresh ingredients."

Meanwhile, Cade was busy growing up on the other side of the country. Boiled peanuts, gooey macaroni and cheese, and deep-fried everything was the love language of the South. Throw in a little football, and you've got yourself a very happy Cade. Cade was quick to learn that every recipe has a story behind it and that the best recipes include a little bit of the cook's soul with the meal.

Fast forward a few years, and somehow we found each other and fell in love with each other and with the flavors of each other's childhoods. We started a life blending not only our traditions and families but also our Pacific Northwest and Southern ways of life.

On our third anniversary, we took a trip to San Francisco, where we tasted the most delicious Margherita pizza ever. It was fresh and flavorful—and the sweet basil was the perfect finishing touch. After returning home, we felt inspired to start cooking with more fresh ingredients, finding new recipes to share, and most of all, doing it together.

It didn't take us long to discover that the more time we shared in the kitchen creating something delicious, the more family stories were discovered and new traditions were created. Our hearts were filled.

Cooking isn't just about the food, it's about the hands that created it. For us, that means sharing a little Southern comfort and a little farm-to-table. But wherever you are and whatever flavors you are sharing, remember that good food and good people make for a good life.

—*Cade and Carrian Cheney*

breakfasts

PERFECT WAFFLES

This is everything we love in a waffle—light, buttery, crisp on the outside, and fluffy on the inside. The secret is to mix the sweet, fresh cream with the Southern-kissed buttermilk. It's like us: a little sweet and a little Southern.

1¾ cups all-purpose flour

2¼ teaspoons baking powder

¼ teaspoon baking soda

2 tablespoons cornstarch

3 tablespoons plus 1 teaspoon granulated sugar

½ teaspoon fine sea salt

3 large eggs

¾ cup buttermilk

¾ cup heavy cream

½ cup (1 stick) unsalted butter, melted and cooled slightly

Heat a waffle iron according to manufacturer's directions.

In a large bowl, whisk together the flour, baking powder, baking soda, cornstarch, sugar, and salt.

In another bowl, whisk together the eggs, buttermilk, and heavy cream.

Using a wooden spoon, stir the wet ingredients into the dry ingredients until just a few streaks of flour remain and the batter is almost mixed together. Add the melted butter and stir until just combined.

Let batter rest 15 to 30 minutes.

Brush butter on both sides of the hot waffle iron. Pour 1 cup batter into the iron and allow to cook per manufacturer's instructions.

Makes 4 waffles.

TIP: Omitting the cornstarch creates a waffle that is crisp on the outside but soft in the middle. Our kids like it with the cornstarch so the waffles are soft and fluffy throughout.

APPLE-BACON CHEDDAR WAFFLES WITH APPLE BUTTER SYRUP

We love recipes that bring my Pacific Northwest roots together with Cade's South Carolina roots, and what better way than to stuff a waffle with bacon and cheese and top it all off with an apple syrup?

1¾ cups all-purpose flour

2¼ teaspoons baking powder

¼ teaspoon baking soda

2 tablespoons cornstarch

3 tablespoons plus 1 teaspoon granulated sugar

½ teaspoon fine sea salt

3 large eggs

¾ cup buttermilk

¾ cup heavy cream

½ cup (1 stick) unsalted butter, melted and cooled slightly

8 slices cheddar cheese

6 slices Applewood smoked bacon, cooked crisp and crumbled

Apple Butter Syrup

Heat a waffle iron according to manufacturer's directions.

In a large bowl, whisk together the flour, baking powder, baking soda, cornstarch, sugar, and salt.

In another bowl, whisk together the eggs, buttermilk, and heavy cream.

Using a wooden spoon, stir the wet ingredients into the dry ingredients until just a few streaks of flour remain and the batter is almost mixed together. Add the melted butter and stir until just combined.

Allow batter to rest 15 to 30 minutes.

Brush butter on both sides of the hot waffle iron. Pour about ⅓ cup of the batter onto the iron, quickly add 1 to 2 pieces of sliced cheese and 1 heaping tablespoon of bacon crumbles, then scoop and gently but quickly spread a little more batter over the top. Cook according to waffle iron instructions.

Serve warm with Apple Butter Syrup.

Makes 4 waffles.

APPLE BUTTER SYRUP

1 granny smith apple, peeled and diced

1 teaspoon olive oil

¼ cup (½ stick) butter

½ cup buttermilk

½ cup apple cider

¾ cup granulated sugar

½ teaspoon ground cinnamon

2 tablespoons Karo Syrup

½ teaspoon baking soda

In a large, heavy pot (not a regular saucepan) over medium heat, add the apples and oil and sauté until soft, about 2 minutes, stirring occasionally.

Add the butter, buttermilk, apple cider, sugar, cinnamon, and Karo Syrup. Bring to a boil. Remove from heat and stir in the baking soda.

Place back on the burner and turn down to a simmer for 3 minutes, or until slightly thickened. Serve immediately.

MELT-IN-YOUR-MOUTH BUTTERMILK PANCAKES WITH BUTTERMILK SYRUP

We spent months testing pancake recipes until we ended up with the fluffiest, Southern-inspired pancake around. The extra thick batter melts beautifully into the perfect pancake! Every weekend it's the most popular recipe on our site. Don't forget to serve it with Buttermilk Syrup!

1 teaspoon salt

2 teaspoons baking powder

1 teaspoon baking soda

2 cups sifted all-purpose flour

2 tablespoons granulated sugar

2 eggs, slightly whisked

2 cups buttermilk

2 tablespoons unsalted butter, melted

Buttermilk Syrup

Preheat a griddle to medium heat.

In a medium bowl, whisk together the salt, baking powder, baking soda, flour, and sugar.

In a separate bowl, whisk together the eggs and buttermilk. Drizzle in the butter as you continue to whisk.

Switch to a wooden spoon and make a well in the middle of the dry ingredients. Pour in the wet ingredients and stir until almost completely combined. The more you stir pancakes, the more flat and tough they will be, so mix gently until a few streaks of flour are remaining.

Butter the griddle and pour on ⅓ cup of the batter, gently spreading the batter into a circle as it will be very thick. Cook until one or two bubbles begin to form on top of the pancake, then flip and cook until golden brown. Serve immediately.

Makes 8 to 10 pancakes.

BUTTERMILK SYRUP

½ cup (1 stick) unsalted butter

1 cup granulated sugar

1 cup buttermilk

2 teaspoons vanilla

1 tablespoon light Karo Syrup

½ teaspoon baking soda

In a large pot or saucepan over medium heat, combine butter, sugar, buttermilk, vanilla, and Karo Syrup. (Use a very large pot to prepare the syrup, as it foams and rises once the baking soda is added.)

Heat until mixture is well combined and comes to a boil.

Quickly remove the pot from the heat and add the baking soda while whisking. Return to the heat, stirring constantly. The syrup will grow large and threaten to boil over, which is why a large pot is essential. If the mixture comes too close to the edge, remove pot from the burner and continue stirring to bring it down. Return to heat and stir 30 to 60 seconds. Remove from heat if it threatens to boil over again. Serve immediately. Refrigerate remaining syrup in an airtight jar for up to 1 week.

PUMPKIN SPICE PANCAKES WITH CINNAMON SYRUP

Pumpkin recipes aren't just for the fall and holiday seasons. We love the flavor all year round, and this particular pumpkin pancake is seriously melt-in-your-mouth divine! Serve it up as is with Cinnamon Syrup and fresh whipped cream, or throw some chocolate chips into the batter!

1 teaspoon salt

2 teaspoons baking powder

1 teaspoon baking soda

1 cup sifted all-purpose flour

1 cup whole wheat flour

2 tablespoons granulated sugar

2 large eggs, slightly whisked

2 cups buttermilk

½ cup pumpkin puree

2 tablespoons unsalted butter, melted

Cinnamon Syrup

Preheat a griddle to medium heat.

In a medium bowl, whisk together the salt, baking powder, baking soda, flours, and sugar.

In a separate bowl, whisk together the eggs, buttermilk, and pumpkin. Drizzle in the butter as you continue to whisk.

Switch to a wooden spoon and make a well in the middle of the dry ingredients. Pour in the wet ingredients and stir until almost completely combined. The more you stir pancakes, the more flat and tough they will be, so mix gently until a few streaks of flour are remaining and the batter is thick and slightly lumpy.

Butter the griddle and pour on a ⅓ cup of the batter. Cook until bubbles begin to form on top of the pancake, then flip and cook until golden brown. Serve immediately with Cinnamon Syrup.

Makes 8 to 10 pancakes.

CINNAMON SYRUP

½ cup (1 stick) butter

1½ cups granulated sugar

¾ cup buttermilk

2 tablespoons light Karo Syrup

1 tablespoon vanilla

¾ teaspoon ground cinnamon (or to taste)

1 teaspoon baking soda

In a large pot over medium heat, add the butter, sugar, buttermilk, and Karo Syrup. Whisk as everything melts together and begins to boil. Allow to boil 5 to 10 minutes, or until mixture begins to thicken.

Add the vanilla and cinnamon and whisk quickly.

Very quickly add the baking soda and continue to whisk. The syrup should seize up and be very bubbly. Allow to cook, boiling, for 2 more minutes; reduce heat to low and keep warm until serving.

The syrup can be kept in an airtight container or jar for up to 2 weeks.

Carrian's Cream-Filled Berry Crepes

CADE'S CLASSIC CREPES

Cade and the girls have a special Saturday tradition of making crepes together. Since crepes aren't difficult to make and come together pretty quickly, they love to top them with all kinds of delicious flavor combinations: berries and chocolate hazelnut spread, berries and whipped cream, bananas and cinnamon, jams or fruit preserves, peanut butter, or even just a light sprinkle of sugar—which is how Carrian likes them.

¾ cup all-purpose flour

2 tablespoons granulated sugar

1¼ cups whole milk

1 large egg plus 1 egg yolk

2 tablespoons butter, melted

In a medium bowl, whisk together the flour and sugar.

In another bowl, whisk together the milk and eggs.

Slowly whisk the wet ingredients into the dry ingredients and then drizzle in the butter until smooth. Allow batter to sit for 15 minutes.

Heat a skillet over medium heat with a little butter or nonstick spray in the pan. Pour ¼ to ⅓ cup of the batter into the pan, lift pan off the burner, and swirl with your wrist so batter covers the entire bottom of the pan. Return the pan to the burner.

Once the edges of the crepe start to lift and curl, carefully flip the crepe. We prefer to use a rubber spatula since it bends and slides right under the crepe. Set crepe aside on a paper-towel lined plate and repeat, using all of the batter.

Serve with your favorite toppings or fillings, such as Nutella, berries, bananas, or jams.

Makes 8 to 12 crepes.

CARRIAN'S CREAM-FILLED BERRY CREPES

2 cups sliced strawberries

2 cups frozen marionberries or blackberries

1 cup brown sugar

½ teaspoon vanilla

1 (8-ounce) package light cream cheese, softened

½ cup powdered sugar

Pinch salt

1 teaspoon lemon juice

1 batch Cade's Classic Crepes, prepared

Combine the berries in a food processor or blender and blend until smooth.

Pour pureed berries in a medium saucepan and warm over low heat. Add brown sugar and vanilla and bring to a simmer.

Reduce heat and keep warm while preparing cream filling.

In a bowl with an electric hand mixer, beat together the cream cheese, powdered sugar, salt, and lemon until smooth, about 2 minutes.

Spread a generous spoonful of cream filling over crepe, roll up, and serve topped with warm berry sauce.

PEACH COBBLER BAKED FRENCH TOAST

There aren't many things better than peach season. One year we ended up with a couple huge boxes and decided to do a mashup of a French toast casserole and our favorite peach cobbler recipe. Let's just say it didn't last long on the breakfast table. This is best prepared the day before serving. Store in the refrigerator, pull out first thing in the morning, bake, and enjoy! Perfect for holidays or when you'll have guests staying the night.

½ loaf French bread, torn in pieces

4 eggs

1 teaspoon plus 1 pinch ground cinnamon, divided

½ cup milk

½ cup sweetened condensed milk

2 large peaches, sliced

1½ cups plus 1 tablespoon all-purpose flour, divided

⅓ cup plus 2 tablespoons brown sugar, divided

9 tablespoons cold butter, cut in small pieces

¼ cup granulated sugar

Grease a 9x13-inch baking pan or an 8x8-inch deep-dish casserole. Scatter torn bread pieces along the bottom of the dish.

In a medium bowl, combine the eggs, ½ teaspoon of the cinnamon, the milk, and the sweetened condensed milk. Whisk to combine and then pour evenly over the bread; set aside.

In a medium saucepan over medium heat, combine sliced peaches, 1 tablespoon of the flour, 2 tablespoons of the brown sugar, and a pinch of cinnamon. Cook and stir 3 minutes, or until tender and saucy in appearance but with peach slices still intact. Remove from heat and allow to cool while you make the topping.

In a large bowl, whisk together the remaining 1½ cups flour, the remaining ⅓ cup brown sugar, the granulated sugar, and ½ teaspoon cinnamon. With a fork or pastry cutter, cut in the butter until it's well incorporated. (When you grab a handful in your hand, it should stick together like wet sand.)

Spread the peach sauce and the crumb topping over the bread mixture and cover the dish with foil.

Refrigerate overnight.

When ready to serve, preheat oven to 350 degrees F. Remove the foil and bake 45 minutes.

Serve with fresh whipped cream and/or Buttermilk Syrup (see recipe on page 5).

Serves 8 to 10.

SAUSAGE BREAKFAST CAKE WITH MAPLE BUTTER SAUCE

In the Pacific Northwest, where Carrian is from, there are a lot of coffee shops, and while we don't drink coffee, we definitely enjoy coffee cake. Cade, on the other hand, has Southern roots, which means he grew up on savory breakfasts. This recipe combines both of our worlds for an amazing sausage breakfast cake.

1 pound ground maple sausage

Vegetable or canola oil

½ yellow onion, diced

1½ cups chopped red and yellow bell peppers

2 cups all-purpose flour

1 tablespoon baking powder

2 tablespoons shortening

¼ teaspoon ground black pepper

¾ teaspoon salt

1 cup shredded Mexican cheese blend or any favorite cheese

1 egg, beaten

¾ cup buttermilk

¼ cup sour cream

¼ cup pure maple syrup

¼ cup (½ stick) butter

Preheat oven to 350 degrees F. Coat an 8x9-inch baking pan with nonstick cooking spray.

In a skillet over medium heat, add the sausage and cook until browned, stirring occasionally to break up the meat, about 3 to 5 minutes. Remove to a mesh strainer in the sink to allow the grease to drain off.

Place the skillet back on the burner (no need to wash it first), add a drizzle of oil, and then add the onion and peppers. Cook, stirring occasionally, for 3 minutes or until the onions are soft and translucent. Remove to a plate to cool.

In a bowl, add the flour, baking powder, shortening, pepper, and salt. Using a pastry cutter or fork, blend the shortening into the flour. Mix in the shredded cheese.

In a small bowl, whisk together the egg, buttermilk, and sour cream.

Create a well in the middle of the dry ingredients and add the egg mixture. Add the sausage and peppers on top and stir until just combined.

Spread the very thick, sticky batter into the baking dish and bake 40 to 45 minutes or until set in the middle and golden brown.

Meanwhile, melt the butter and maple syrup together in a small pan and set aside.

Remove the cake from the oven and allow to cool for a few minutes; pour the sauce all over the top and serve immediately.

Serves 6 to 8.

HASH BROWNS HAM FRITTATA

There's something wonderful about golden, crispy hash browns, and we just couldn't resist making a crust out of them for this frittata. Crispy hashed browns with a cheesy egg and juicy ham filling is a breakfast pretty enough for Mother's Day but easy enough for any weekend.

Vegetable or canola oil

4 cups hash browns, divided

Salt

Ground black pepper

10 large eggs

¼ cup milk

½ teaspoon salt

¼ teaspoon pepper

1 cup shredded cheddar cheese

1 cup chopped mini sweet peppers

½ cup chopped green bell pepper

1½ cups chopped smoked or brown sugar ham

1½ cups baby spinach

Preheat oven to 375 degrees F.

For the crust, heat a nonstick skillet over medium heat. Add about ¼ cup oil. Once hot, add half of the hash browns. Sprinkle with salt and pepper and allow to cook 7 to 8 minutes. Flip the hash browns once golden and cook an additional 2 to 4 minutes, or until golden. Remove hash browns from pan and set aside. Repeat with remaining hash browns.

In a separate, oven-safe skillet or cast-iron skillet, drizzle a small amount of oil in the bottom and rub it around with a napkin. Lay half of the cooked hash browns in the bottom to cover the entire surface. Press the remaining hash browns along the sides of the skillet to create a crust. Set aside.

In a large bowl, whisk together the eggs, milk, salt, and pepper. Stir in the cheese and set aside.

Heat the empty nonstick skillet to medium-high and add the chopped peppers. Cook for 2 minutes or until tender, stirring occasionally. Add the ham and spinach and cook another 2 minutes, or until the spinach has cooked down completely; set aside.

Return the skillet with the hash browns crust to the hot burner. Let the potatoes begin to heat up again, about 1 minute.

In the meantime, quickly combine the pepper and ham mixture with the egg and cheese mixture and then pour it over the crust in the skillet. Allow to cook for about 30 seconds, or until the sides just begin to set.

Move the pan to the preheated oven and bake 10 to 12 minutes, or until the middle is set and does not jiggle when moved. Allow to cool 5 minutes before serving.

Serves 4 to 6.

STRAWBERRY-ALMOND GRANOLA

A good batch of granola is a must in every Washington household, and we happen to think that ours is the ultimate recipe. You can change out the nuts or Craisins for any nut or dried fruit. The secret to these yummy clusters is to make sure you pile up the granola on the pan to bake, then let it cool completely before breaking it up into chunks.

½ **cup coconut oil**

½ **cup real maple syrup**

2 **tablespoons brown sugar**

1 **tablespoon honey**

1 **tablespoon vanilla**

3½ **cups rolled oats (not quick)**

1 **teaspoon salt**

1½ **teaspoons ground cinnamon**

1 **cup sliced almonds**

¼ **cup pumpkin seeds**

1 **egg white, whisked until foamy**

1 **cup strawberry-flavored Craisins**

Preheat oven to 325 degrees F. Line a 9x13-inch pan with parchment paper.

In a medium saucepan over medium heat, add the coconut oil, maple syrup, brown sugar, and honey. Cook until everything is combined, stirring occasionally.

Remove from heat and stir in the vanilla.

In a very large bowl, stir together the oats, salt, cinnamon, almonds, and pumpkin seeds.

Pour the hot syrup over the granola and stir to combine.

Add the egg white and fold in.

Spread the granola over the parchment-lined baking pan and bake 35 to 45 minutes or until lightly golden. Remove from the oven and allow to cool completely.

Once completely cooled, break the granola up and toss with the Craisins. Store in mason jars for up to one month.

Makes 2 quarts.

BREAKFAST FRUIT PIZZA

It's no secret that Carrian loves granola and fresh fruit, and Cade could eat pizza every day and never get sick of it, so clearly we were meant to make a breakfast pizza. Our kids love making designs with the fruit. Use any fruit you like and feel free to try different flavors of cream cheese and yogurt as well. Depending on the size of your crust, use more or less fruit.

1 batch Strawberry-Almond Granola, prepared without the egg white and Craisins (see recipe on page 17)

1 (8-ounce) carton whipped mixed berry cream cheese

1 (5.3-ounce) carton vanilla Greek yogurt

½ teaspoon lemon zest

1 tablespoon lemon juice

1 mango, peeled and sliced

1 pint strawberries, washed and sliced

1 pint blackberries, washed and sliced

1½ cups grapes, sliced

1 pint raspberries

Preheat oven to 325 degrees F. and line a pizza stone or baking sheet with parchment paper.

Prepare Strawberry-Almond Granola as instructed on page 17 though without the egg white and strawberry Craisins.

Press the granola onto prepared pan in a thick circle. Bake 35 to 45 minutes and remove to cool.

Meanwhile, in a large bowl, stir together the cream cheese, yogurt, lemon zest, and juice.

Once the crust is cool, spread cream cheese layer over the bottom of the pizza, leaving the edges bare.

Arrange the fruit over the top of the cream cheese mixture, cut pizza into slices, and serve. You can also wrap pizza loosely with plastic wrap and store up to 6 hours in the refrigerator before serving.

Serves 4 to 6.

TIP: To keep your cream cheese smooth, bring to room temperature before mixing.

BLACKBERRY CRISP BAKED OATMEAL

Years ago, if you would have told us that mornings would be our favorite time of day we would have laughed, but it's true! There's not much we'd rather do than start our days together as a family with blackberry crisp baked oatmeal.

3 cups old fashioned oats

2 teaspoons baking powder

½ teaspoon salt

1 large egg

2 cups skim milk

¼ cup coconut oil, melted

⅓ cup apple butter

¼ cup granulated sugar

1 cup brown sugar, divided

2 tablespoons whole wheat flour

2 tablespoons all-purpose flour

½ cup walnuts or pecans, chopped fine

¼ cup (½ stick) cold butter

½ teaspoon ground cinnamon

2 cups frozen blackberries

Heavy cream or yogurt for garnish

Preheat oven to 400 degrees F. and coat an 8x8-inch baking pan with nonstick spray.

In a medium bowl, stir together the oats, baking powder, and salt.

In a large bowl, whisk together the egg, milk, coconut oil, apple butter, granulated sugar, and ¼ cup of the brown sugar. Stir in the oats.

Pour mixture into prepared baking dish and bake 20 minutes.

While mixture bakes, prepare a crumb topping by combining remaining ingredients, except berries, in a small bowl.

Remove mixture from oven and carefully fold in frozen berries. Top with prepared crumb topping and bake an additional 18 to 20 minutes, or until the top is golden in color.

Drizzle with cream or a dollop of yogurt to serve.

Serves 4 to 6.

WHOLE WHEAT BLUEBERRY MUFFINS

Growing up, one of Carrian's favorite muffin flavors was chocolate. Now that she's older, she feels a little guilty eating something that tastes more like a cupcake than a muffin for breakfast so she tends to make fruit-filled muffins. One morning, Cade accidentally added strawberry Greek yogurt to the mix, and we've been doing it that way ever since. These muffins are light, fluffy, and have a wonderful flavor, but it's the crunchy sugar on top that we really love.

¼ cup strawberry Greek yogurt

¼ cup coconut oil, melted

¼ cup honey

½ cup brown sugar

½ cup milk

½ teaspoon vanilla

½ cup oat flour

1 cup whole wheat flour

2 teaspoons baking powder

½ teaspoon baking soda

½ teaspoon salt

½ cup all-purpose flour

1½ cups blueberries

Turbinado sugar, for topping

Preheat oven to 425 degrees F. and line a jumbo-sized muffin tin with paper liners, or grease well.

In a bowl with an electric mixer, blend the yogurt and coconut oil. Add honey, sugar, milk, and vanilla and mix again until smooth.

In a separate bowl, whisk together the dry ingredients, with the exception of the all-purpose flour.

Toss the berries in the all-purpose flour. Shake off excess flour and place flour-covered berries in another bowl. Add remaining flour to the dry ingredients.

With the mixer on, slowly add the dry ingredients to the wet ingredients and mix until smooth.

Remove bowl from mixer and, using a spatula, fold berries into the batter. Fill muffin cups ⅔ full. Top with turbinado sugar and bake 15 to 20 minutes, or until golden on top.

Makes 6 to 9 jumbo muffins.

CHOCOLATE CHIP ZUCCHINI BANANA BREAD

Chocolate plus vegetables plus banana bread? Sounds like a crazy mashup of flavors, but trust us—it's amazing. In fact, it might be the most delicious and moist banana bread we've ever had.

1½ cups all-purpose flour

1 teaspoon baking soda

½ teaspoon baking powder

1¼ teaspoons cream of tartar

½ teaspoon salt

½ cup canola oil

⅔ cup granulated sugar

1 large egg, slightly beaten

1 cup finely grated zucchini (about 1 medium zucchini)

1 cup mashed banana (about 2 large bananas)

1½ cups chocolate chips

Preheat oven to 350 degrees F. and grease an 8½x4-inch loaf pan.

In a medium bowl, whisk together the flour, baking soda, baking powder, cream of tartar, and salt. Set aside.

In the bowl of an electric stand mixer, beat together the canola oil and sugar. Add the egg and mix again. Dump in the zucchini and mix on medium speed until everything is evenly combined.

Starting and ending with the flour mixture, alternate adding the flour and mashed banana a little at a time while the mixer runs on low.

Fold in the chocolate chips and pour batter into prepared loaf pan.

Bake 50 to 55 minutes, tenting with foil the last 15 minutes to avoid too much browning. Allow bread to cool before slicing, then serve warmed up with a little butter.

Makes 1 loaf.

HEIRLOOM APPLE ROLLS

This recipe for apple rolls has been passed down through Carrian's family for more than two hundred years. Her grandma is one of the sweetest people we know, and we love to hear her stories about her childhood. Family recipes help us feel close to those who came before us and keep their memories alive in us.

2 cups all-purpose flour

4 teaspoons baking powder

½ teaspoon salt

¼ cup (½ stick) chilled shortening or butter, diced

¾ cup milk

2 tablespoons butter, melted

2 teaspoons ground cinnamon

¼ cup brown sugar

3 cups grated apples (about 3 to 4 apples)

1 cup granulated sugar

2 cups water

Preheat oven to 400 degrees F.

In a large bowl, whisk together the flour, baking powder, and salt.

Add the shortening or butter pieces and cut in with a pastry cutter or fork until the mixture becomes sand-like in texture (the shortening or butter should be pea-sized). Add the milk and stir to form a soft dough.

On a floured board, roll the dough in an oblong sheet ¼-inch thick, and brush with melted butter.

Combine cinnamon and brown sugar in a small bowl.

Cover dough with grated apples and sprinkle with cinnamon-sugar mixture. Set aside.

In a medium saucepan over medium heat, combine the water and sugar to create a simple syrup. Heat through and stir until sugar is completely dissolved. Pour mixture into a 9x13-inch baking dish.

Roll dough out jelly roll style, cut in slices 1½-inches thick, and place cut side down in the pan of sugar water.

Bake 40 minutes or until the rolls have enlarged to fill the entire pan. Serve warm in a bowl with milk or cream.

Makes 8 to 12 rolls.

DOUBLE CHOCOLATE BANANA MUFFINS

Our youngest daughter is obsessed with banana bread. When she sees bananas on the counter, she won't let anyone else eat them so they can ripen enough to make her favorite treat. So, of course, we had to mashup a recipe for double chocolate banana muffins. It is simple and delicious, and may just be your new obsession.

¼ cup plus 1 teaspoon cocoa powder

1¾ cups all-purpose flour

½ teaspoon baking soda

2 teaspoons baking powder

½ teaspoon cream of tartar

¼ teaspoon salt

⅓ cup shortening or butter, softened

⅔ cup granulated sugar

2 large eggs

½ teaspoon vanilla

1 cup mashed bananas (about 2 medium bananas)

1½ cups semisweet chocolate chips

Preheat oven to 375 degrees F. and line a jumbo muffin tin with paper cupcake liners. (If you use a regular muffin tin, note different baking time below.)

In a medium bowl, whisk together the cocoa, flour, baking soda, baking powder, cream of tartar, and salt; set aside.

In a large mixing bowl with an electric mixer, beat the shortening, sugar, eggs, and vanilla until smooth.

Slowly add a little of the flour mixture to the creamed mixture and stir. Add a little of the mashed banana, mix, and continue to alternate dry ingredients and banana, ending with the banana.

Fold in the chocolate chips. Spoon batter into muffin tins, filling each cup ⅔ full.

Bake 25 to 30 minutes and allow to cool. For regular muffins, bake 14 to 18 minutes.

Makes 6 jumbo muffins or 12 to 16 regular muffins.

SPICED BREAKFAST COOKIES

Cookies for breakfast! That's our kids' favorite thing to hear. Well, that and Crepe Saturday! (Nothing beats Cade's Classic Crepes at our house on a Saturday morning.) These spiced breakfast cookies are great for busy mornings or an afternoon soccer game. And to be honest, Carrian totally snacks on them while the kids are at school. Hey, moms like snacks, too!

1⅓ cups raw whole almonds or ¾ cup almond butter

2 overripe bananas

¼ cup real maple syrup

1 tablespoon molasses

½ teaspoon dried orange zest

1 teaspoon ground cinnamon

¼ teaspoon ground nutmeg

¼ teaspoon ground cloves

¼ teaspoon ground ginger

2¼ cups old fashioned oats

¾ cup white chocolate chips (optional)

½ cup Craisins or raisins (optional)

Preheat oven to 350 degrees F. and line a baking sheet with parchment paper or coat with nonstick cooking spray.

In a heavy-duty blender, process the almonds to create a thick almond butter. If almond butter becomes too warm during processing, set it aside to cool so the cookies will bake properly.

In a large bowl, combine ¾ cup almond butter with the bananas, maple syrup, molasses, orange zest, and spices. Mix, mashing the bananas as you stir, so that they are well incorporated but small chunks remain.

Add the oats, chocolate chips, and Craisins and fold everything together.

Using a cookie dough scoop or two spoons, scoop the dough into balls on the cookie sheet. Press the tops gently to flatten them out, as these cookies will not spread at all during baking.

Bake 10 minutes and serve warm. Or cool on wire racks, place in a sealed container, and store in the refrigerator up to 1 week.

Makes 16 to 20 cookies.

GREEN SMOOTHIE PROTEIN PARFAIT

For years we refused to try Cade's green smoothies and protein shakes, but then he put the two together, and we all wanted seconds. Not only is it good for you, but it's fresh, flavorful, creamy, and helps keep you full all morning long.

½ cup milk (almond, rice or coconut milk are fine too)

1 cup spinach

½ cup frozen mango chunks

¼ cup frozen banana slices

4 almonds

1 scoop vanilla protein powder

½ cup granola (See page 17 for our favorite granola recipe)

3 slices banana

In a blender, in this order, add the milk, spinach, mango, frozen bananas, almonds, and protein powder.

Blend until completely smooth and then pour in a parfait dish or glass.

Top with ½ cup granola and 3 banana slices.

Serves 1.

soups and salads

TACO STEW

"Is it a stew or a chili?" That's the most commonly asked question we get about this recipe, and to be honest, we don't know! Whichever you call it, just try it because it is one of the yummiest dinners for those crisp, chilly fall nights.

2 teaspoons olive oil

1 onion, chopped

3 to 4 carrots, peeled and diced

4 medium russet potatoes, peeled and diced

1 pound ground beef

1 (16-ounce) bag frozen peas

1 (16-ounce) can diced tomatoes

1 (8-ounce) can tomato sauce

1 (1.75-ounce) envelope taco seasoning

1 (15-ounce) can corn, undrained

1 (15-ounce) can chili beans, undrained

1 (15-ounce) can green beans, undrained

1 (15-ounce) can kidney beans, undrained

Toppings: shredded cheese, sour cream, corn chips

Heat a drizzle of olive oil in a large pot over medium heat. Add onion and cook until tender, about 3 minutes. Add the carrots and potatoes and just enough water to cover them. Cook until tender.

In a separate pan over medium heat, brown the ground beef, drain off the fat, and add cooked meat to the water and tender veggies.

Add remaining ingredients and cook until heated through.

Serve with shredded cheese, sour cream, and chips.

Serves 8.

SWEET-POTATO APPLE TURKEY CHILI

Carrian writes, "I love it when my house smells like made-from-scratch soup and hot homemade bread. It reminds me of my childhood home and time spent with my mother. I get such a thrill out of creating those same feelings in our home. Whether it's the girls coming home from school or Cade walking in the door from work, there's nothing better than hearing, 'What smells so amazing?' This mashup chili recipe will absolutely make your house smell like . . . well, like home."

1 large sweet potato, baked and peeled (bake about at 400 degrees F. for 45 minutes)

3 cups chicken or vegetable broth

1 tablespoon olive oil

1 large carrot, chopped

½ red bell pepper, chopped

½ yellow bell pepper, chopped

1 zucchini, chopped

½ pound lean ground turkey

1 large apple, peeled and chopped

1 cup skim milk

¼ teaspoon pumpkin pie spice

Salt to taste, start with ½ teaspoon

In a blender, puree baked sweet potato and the broth until smooth; set aside.

Heat oil in a large pot over medium heat. Add the carrots, peppers, and zucchini and sauté until tender, about 5 minutes.

Add the ground turkey and apple and cook through, about 5 to 8 more minutes.

Once everything is cooked through and tender, add the puree and milk to the pot, stirring gently to lift any browned bits from the bottom of the pan.

Add pumpkin pie spice and salt to taste and reduce heat to a simmer. Simmer at least 30 minutes—and up to several hours—prior to serving. Taste and balance flavors with extra salt, if needed, before serving.

Serve with potato rolls (page 94) or sweet potato rolls (page 97).

Serves 6.

CHICKEN POT PIE SOUP WITH BUTTERMILK BISCUITS

Cade loves a good Southern "chicken and dumplings," and Carrian can make a mean pot pie, stuffed full of chicken and veggies. So naturally we combined the recipes into a soup with homemade buttermilk biscuits on top. It was so good that Cade has a new favorite "dumplin'" recipe now.

You can make this in the morning and allow it to cool slightly before placing in the fridge. Then, for dinner, all it requires is to reheat it. The flavors really do get better throughout the day without needing to boil the soup too much.

For a lighter version, use milk instead of half-and-half and cream or a combination.

1 tablespoon olive oil

1 onion, minced

2 cloves garlic, minced

5 teaspoons roughly chopped fresh thyme

1 tablespoon chopped fresh parsley

2 Yukon gold potatoes, chopped in ¼-inch pieces

1 heaping tablespoon all-purpose flour

2 cups half-and-half

2 cups chicken broth or stock

1 cup heavy cream

1 bay leaf

2 teaspoons kosher salt

½ teaspoon freshly ground black pepper

3 cups cooked, shredded chicken

1 (12-ounce) bag frozen peas and carrots

Buttermilk biscuits, prepared

Heat oil in a large Dutch oven or soup pot over medium heat until it begins to shimmer. Add the onion and cook 2 to 3 minutes, or until translucent and tender. Add the garlic, thyme, parsley, and potatoes and cook an additional 30 seconds, stirring once or twice.

Quickly whisk in flour and cook another 30 seconds, stirring continuously.

Pour in the half-and-half, chicken stock, cream, and bay leaf and bring to a boil.

Reduce heat to low, season with salt and pepper, add the chicken and veggies and simmer 30 minutes, or up to 2 hours, checking often to ensure the liquid does not cook off. If preparing ahead of time, simmer for only 30 minutes before cooling and refrigerating.

Remove bay leaf, adjust seasonings if needed, and serve with warm, pre-made buttermilk biscuits, cut into squares.

Serves 6.

CREAMY BUTTERNUT SQUASH TORTELLINI SOUP

This soup is one of our favorites for fall. We love the hint of sweet flavor from the sweet potato and carrots, and the dash of lemon pepper brightens up the earthy flavor. And the tortellini floating inside are like buried treasures. It's what every winter soup dreams of being.

1 medium to large butternut squash

Olive oil

Salt and pepper

1 sweet potato

20 baby carrots

2 cloves garlic

3 cups chicken or vegetable broth

2 cups heavy cream

1¼ teaspoons lemon pepper

2 tablespoons brown sugar

1 to 2 teaspoons salt

¼ cup fresh chopped parsley

1 (7-ounce) box cheese tortellini

Preheat oven to 350 degrees F.

Cut open the squash, place it on a baking sheet, and drizzle with olive oil, salt, and pepper. Add sweet potato and carrots to baking sheet, rolling the carrots in any oil and salt that ended up on the pan.

Bake 30 minutes, remove the carrots, and continue to bake an additional 30 to 45, minutes or until the sweet potato and squash are tender. Allow to cool slightly.

Scoop the meat out of the squash and the sweet potato and place in a blender. Add the carrots and garlic and puree until smooth. You may add a little of the broth if your blender needs help making the mixture smooth.

In a large pot over medium heat, pour in the pureed squash mixture, broth, cream, lemon pepper, and brown sugar. Stir well and bring to a simmer.

Reduce heat to low and season soup with 1 teaspoon of the salt. Taste and add more salt only if needed. Add parsley and allow to simmer 20 to 30 minutes.

Meanwhile, prepare tortellini according to package directions.

To serve, add the tortellini to soup in the pot and cook for another 2 minutes to bring everything to the same temperature; serve immediately.

Serves 6 to 8.

GOLDEN LOADED BAKED POTATO SOUP

Carrian's mom always—literally every single time—served cinnamon rolls with potato soup. Years later she asked her mom what she was thinking serving dessert with the soup, and she said it was because the kids refused to eat it so the rolls were her method of bribery. We've taken Mom's recipe and made it our own, but we still include her secret: a drizzle of honey. Trust us on this one.

Just so you know, using Yukon gold potatoes makes this the creamiest potato soup you'll ever gobble up.

5 medium to large Yukon gold potatoes, cut in half

2 tablespoons unsalted butter

2 teaspoons Better than Bouillon Roasted Chicken Base

1 small onion, chopped fine

2 tablespoons all-purpose flour

3 cups skim milk

2 cups heavy cream or half-and-half

¼ cup sour cream plus more for topping

1 to 2 tablespoons honey plus more for drizzling

Kosher salt to taste

Pepper to taste

6 slices bacon, cooked crisp and crumbled

Shredded extra sharp cheese

Place potatoes in a large stockpot and cover with water. Heat over medium-high and cook just until potatoes are fork tender. Drain water off the potatoes, peel off the skins, and chop in to bite-sized pieces. Mash about ¾ of the chopped potatoes and set aside with chopped potatoes.

Add butter and chicken stock or base to the stockpot. Whisk until butter is melted and then add onion. Cook until translucent, about 3 to 4 minutes.

Quickly whisk in the flour and stir continuously for 1 minute. The mixture should be clumpy and golden in color.

Add the milk and cream, whisking as you pour to dissolve the lumps. Bring the mixture to a boil. Reduce heat and simmer until soup begins to thicken, about 5 to 10 minutes.

Add the sour cream, honey, and salt and pepper to taste. Add reserved potatoes and continue to cook 5 to 10 minutes.

Serve in bowls, topped with cheese, bacon, sour cream, and a drizzle of honey.

Serves 4 to 6.

FABULOUS OVEN STEW

We love reinventing old recipes, and at our house we call this one "Mom's fabulous oven stew" because not only is it fabulous, but it can go in either the slow cooker or the oven. It's practically the only stew recipe we make anymore.

1 pound stew meat, cubed

⅓ cup butter

1 onion, chopped

2 stalks celery, halved lengthwise and diced

5 carrots, peeled and sliced on a bias

¾ cup diced baby Bella mushrooms

⅓ cup all-purpose flour

1½ cups heavy cream

½ cup milk

2 potatoes, chopped but unpeeled

1 (8-ounce) can tomato sauce

1 package dry onion soup mix

2 teaspoons dry basil or 4 teaspoons chopped fresh

1 cups chicken or vegetable broth

Add meat cubes to a large, oven-safe Dutch oven or stockpot over medium-high heat. Cook, stirring only occasionally for about 2 minutes, until the meat is browned on all sides. (There is no need to cook meat through completely.) Remove to a plate and place the pot back on the burner over medium heat.

Add the butter, and when it is almost completely melted, add the onion, celery, carrots, and mushrooms. Stir to combine. Cook 2 to 3 minutes, or until the onions begin to soften and become translucent.

Using a wooden spoon, stir in the flour and allow to cook for 30 seconds. Add the cream and milk and stir to combine. Allow mixture to cook 1 to 3 minutes, or until it begins to thicken.

Add the potatoes, tomato sauce, dry soup mix, basil, and broth.

Cover Dutch oven and place in 250-degree-F. oven for 8 hours. Alternatively, transfer to slow cooker and cook on low 8 hours.

Serve with rolls or bread on the side.

Serves 6.

ROASTED TOMATO BASIL SOUP WITH GRILLED CHEESE CROUTONS

Few foods are as "down-home" as tomato soup with grilled cheese sandwiches. We gave this classic a twist of sophistication using fresh-from-the-garden summer tomatoes and basil. The roasted flavor is amazing, but the real stars of the show are the baby caprese, grilled cheese "croutons," floating in all their gooey, cheesy glory.

4 teaspoons olive oil, plus more for brushing on pan, divided

8 to 12 small to medium vine-ripened tomatoes, quartered

1 teaspoon kosher salt

Freshly ground pepper to taste

3 cups tomato sauce (optional)

2 cloves garlic, minced

2 tablespoons minced onion

1 cup chicken broth

1 tablespoon dark brown sugar

1 cup heavy cream

1 baguette, sliced diagonally into ¼-inch slices

Fresh mozzarella, sliced

Butter, softened

1 tablespoon fresh chopped basil

Preheat oven to 425 degrees F. and brush a large baking sheet with olive oil.

Place the tomatoes on prepared baking sheet and drizzle with 2 teaspoons olive oil. Toss to coat and then sprinkle evenly with kosher salt and black pepper. Roast in oven 20 to 40 minutes, until tomatoes are shriveled and soft.

Remove tomatoes from the oven and let cool slightly. Place tomatoes in blender jar, reserving 1 cup of the juices from the pan. Puree tomatoes in blender until smooth. If needed, add enough canned tomato sauce to equal 3 cups; set aside.

Heat remaining 2 teaspoons olive oil in a large pot over medium-high heat until shimmering. Add the garlic and onion, reduce heat to medium, and stir until fragrant, about 30 seconds.

Add the 3 cups reserved tomato puree, 1 cup reserved tomato juice, chicken broth, brown sugar, and salt and pepper to taste. Stir and bring to a boil. Boil 10 minutes and then reduce to a simmer.

When soup begins to simmer, stir in the cream and simmer 10 to 15 minutes.

Meanwhile, assemble bread slices and mozzarella slices to make mini grilled cheese sandwiches. Butter the outsides of the bread and grill in a nonstick skillet over medium heat until bread is toasted and cheese melts.

Remove from pan and chop into ½- to 1-inch squares.

To serve, fill a bowl with soup, and then top with fresh basil and mini grilled cheese croutons.

Serves 4 to 6.

HONEY-LIME CHICKEN ENCHILADA SOUP

This soup is a delicious twist on one of our favorite chicken enchilada recipes and one of our favorites no matter the weather. Don't skip the tortilla strips—that's the best part!

2 tablespoons chili powder

⅓ cup honey

4 cloves garlic, minced, divided

¼ cup freshly squeezed lime juice

2 cups cooked and shredded chicken

1 carrot, washed

1 red bell pepper, stems and seeds removed

½ yellow onion, peeled

Olive oil

1 (35-ounce) can Cento Italian Tomatoes

½ avocado

⅓ cup freshly chopped cilantro

2 tablespoons diced green chiles

1 teaspoon cumin

1 teaspoon salt

¼ teaspoon ground coriander

4 cups chicken stock

1 (14-ounce) can black beans, drained and rinsed

1½ cups frozen sweet corn

2 cups shredded cheddar cheese

Tortilla strips for garnish

Sour cream, optional

Preheat oven to 400 degrees F.

In a small dish, whisk together the chili powder, honey, 2 cloves of garlic, and the lime juice. Add the chicken and toss to coat. Refrigerate while prepping the rest of the ingredients.

Place the carrot, red pepper, and onion on a baking pan, drizzle with a little olive oil, and sprinkle with a pinch of salt; toss to coat. Roast 15 to 20 minutes or until tender.

Place the tomatoes, roasted vegetables, avocado, cilantro, green chiles, remaining garlic, cumin, salt, coriander, and stock in a blender. Blend until completely smooth. You can do this in two batches if your blender is on the smaller side. Alternatively, place ingredients in a large pot and use a handheld immersion blender to puree.

Transfer soup base from blender to a large stockpot. Add chicken with marinade, black beans, and corn. Heat over medium heat until warmed through.

To serve, fill oven-safe bowls with soup, top with cheese, and place under a broiler cheese is melted. Serve with crunchy tortilla strips, and sour cream if desired.

Serves 6.

MANGO CHICKEN SALAD

We know, we know—there's pasta in our salad. But it's awesome; trust us. Cade swears the best mangoes come from Brazil, and this salad has an awesome tropical, Asian, and Italian flair so it's a little bit of everything from everywhere. Not only is it great as a salad, but we often throw some tortillas on the plate and make it a wrap too!

1½ cups light coconut milk, divided

⅓ cup lime juice, divided

¼ cup plus 2 tablespoons reduced-sodium soy sauce, divided

2 boneless, skinless chicken breasts

2 tablespoons peanut butter

2 tablespoons honey

2 cups chopped Napa cabbage

2 cups chopped romaine lettuce

1 cup peeled and chopped jicama

1 cup peeled and chopped mango

1½ cups chopped seedless cucumber

1 red bell pepper, chopped

½ cup chopped strawberries

½ cup peeled and chopped oranges

¼ cup chopped red onion

¼ cup chopped cilantro

1½ cups cooked angel hair pasta, prepared according to package directions

¼ cup slivered almonds, toasted

1 tablespoon chia seeds

To a large Ziploc bag, add 1 cup of the coconut milk, 3 tablespoons lime juice, and 2 tablespoons soy sauce. Add the chicken, seal the bag, and shake gently to coat the chicken. Marinate in the refrigerator for at least 1 hour and up to 6 hours.

In a small mason jar, add the remaining ½ cup coconut milk, lime juice, soy sauce, peanut butter, and honey. Screw on the lid and shake to combine. Store in the fridge.

Heat a grill pan over medium heat and brush with a small amount of olive oil. Remove chicken from the marinade, discarding the marinade, and grill until cooked through, about 12 to 15 minutes, turning once. Let cool slightly, chop, and then set aside.

In a large bowl, combine the cabbage, romaine, jicama, mango, cucumber, bell pepper, strawberries, oranges, red onion, cilantro, pasta, and chopped chicken.

Pour reserved dressing from the mason jar over the salad and toss to coat. Sprinkle with the almonds and chia seeds. Serve immediately.

Serves 6.

7-LAYER SALAD

Fresh peas are so sweet and delicious, and this recipe is one of those classic salads that everyone should have in their rotation. And since Cade loves Southern-style layered salads, we added a few extra ingredients to make it taste like home.

1½ cups mayonnaise

2 tablespoons granulated sugar

½ teaspoon salt

1 teaspoon apple cider vinegar

4 cups chopped romaine lettuce

2 cups chopped tomatoes

6 hard-boiled eggs, chopped

2 cups frozen peas, defrosted

1½ cups cheddar cheese cubes

1 English cucumber, chopped

½ cup shredded cheddar or Colby Jack cheese

6 slices bacon, cooked crisp and crumbled

In a small bowl, whisk together the mayonnaise, sugar, salt, and vinegar. Set aside.

In a large glass bowl or trifle dish, layer the remaining ingredients, with the exception of the shredded cheese and bacon, in the order listed.

Spread reserved dressing over the top. Cover with plastic wrap and refrigerate at least 1 hour and up to 3 hours.

Top with shredded cheese and bacon crumbles and serve!

Serves 6 to 8.

GARDEN BALSAMIC SALAD

Balsamic vinegar is one of our favorite ingredients. We love to make a reduction for tarts, a vinaigrette for salads, or toss it with strawberries and a little sugar for a summer treat. One of our favorite summer sides is this garden-fresh salad. Chop up a variety of peppers, tomatoes, and avocados, whisk together some oil, garlic, and vinegar, then serve it with any main dish, especially anything straight from the grill.

2 cups grape tomatoes, halved

1 cup chopped mini sweet peppers

1 green bell pepper, sliced

1 avocado, chopped

Salt and pepper to taste

¼ cup extra virgin olive oil

2 tablespoons balsamic vinegar

3 cloves garlic, minced

In a large bowl or shallow platter, add all of the veggies and sprinkle with a little salt and pepper.

In a separate, small bowl, whisk together the oil, vinegar, and garlic.

Toss dressing with the veggies and chill 10 to 15 minutes. Gently toss again and serve.

Serves 4 to 6.

STRAWBERRY CUCUMBER SALAD

We love simple side dishes that bring out the natural flavors of the fruit or veggie where we can just let the food do its thing. This strawberry cucumber salad is light, easy, and always a crowd pleaser.

1 pint strawberries, stemmed and sliced

1 large cucumber, roughly peeled and sliced thin

2 tablespoons balsamic vinegar

2 tablespoons honey

Arrange strawberries and cucumbers in a bowl, layering one over the other in a fan shape.

In a small bowl, whisk together balsamic vinegar and honey, then drizzle over sliced berries and cucumbers. Serve immediately.

Serves 4 to 6.

PEA PASTA SALAD

Cade says that the South loves every part of a meal and that sides are just as important as the main dish. And it's true: there's nothing like a big pile of pasta salad next to your fall-off-the-bone ribs to make a meal complete.

8 ounces dry pasta, such as gemelli

1 cup mayonnaise

1 teaspoon apple cider vinegar

1 teaspoon Dijon mustard

1 tablespoon granulated sugar

¼ teaspoon salt

⅛ teaspoon ground black pepper

1 cup frozen peas, defrosted

1 cup chopped tomatoes

1 cup chopped cucumbers

1 green bell pepper, chopped

3 hard-boiled eggs, chopped

1 cup cheddar cheese cubes

4 slices bacon, cooked crisp and crumbled

Cook the pasta according to package directions, being sure to not over-cook it. Drain well and set aside.

In a large bowl, whisk together the mayonnaise, vinegar, mustard, sugar, salt, and pepper.

Stir in the pasta, peas, tomatoes, cucumbers, bell pepper, eggs, and cheese.

Top with bacon crumbles and serve. (If you choose to make this salad ahead of time, stir in the cheese and bacon just before serving.)

Serves 8 to 10.

CAPRESE PISTACHIO SALAD

Fresh-from-the-garden tomatoes and store-bought tomatoes might as well be apples and oranges, they are so different. Whenever we have a few juicy, ripe tomatoes just picked from the vine, we like to layer them up with fresh mozzarella and basil, but lately we've been throwing on chopped pistachios, which takes this dish to a whole new level of deliciousness.

It's also an easy salad to prepare in advance. Simply arrange the tomatoes and cheese on a plate, cover with plastic wrap, and refrigerate. When you're ready to serve, dress the salad and add fresh basil and pistachios. We like to serve the salad with toast points or flatbread to sop up some of the dressing.

3 large tomatoes

1 pound fresh mozzarella

Olive oil

Good quality balsamic vinegar

Salt and pepper

⅓ **cup chopped pistachios**

2 tablespoons chopped fresh basil

Crispy toast points or flatbread
   (optional)

Slice the tomatoes and mozzarella and arrange in a spiral shape in a dish or bowl.

Drizzle with olive oil, balsamic vinegar, and a sprinkle of salt and pepper.

Top with pistachios and basil and serve immediately.

Serves 4 to 6.

FRUIT SALAD WITH LEMON-GINGER DRESSING

Our oldest daughter loves it when we serve fruit salad with a meal, and last year she added some leftover lemon dressing from our favorite spinach salad. It was delicious! The bright, fresh flavors added a tangy twist to this family classic. We love that our kids are starting to love cooking just as much as we do. This recipe is all thanks to her!

1 teaspoon lemon zest

½ cup freshly squeezed lemon juice

¼ cup canola oil

¼ cup granulated sugar

⅛ teaspoon ground ginger

1 (16-ounce) package strawberries, washed, hulled, and sliced

1 pint blueberries

1 pint raspberries

2 mangos, peeled and chopped

2 cups grapes, halved

1 (15-ounce) can mandarin oranges, drained

In a glass measuring cup, whisk together the zest, lemon juice, oil, sugar, and ginger. Set aside.

In a large bowl, add all of the fruit, drizzle with as much or as little dressing as you like, and gently fold everything together until lightly coated. Leftover dressing can be refrigerated for up to a week and used over fruit or green salads as desired.

Serves 4 to 6.

DILL PEA AND CUCUMBER SALAD

Our family loves to go on picnics. In fact, we have two baskets and three blankets so we can invite friends or family and enjoy an afternoon or evening relaxing on the soft grass while everyone chats and the kids play a little soccer or Frisbee. We've found a few simple, refreshing recipes like this dill salad that are perfect for those picturesque evenings—and even for the evenings when we bring out the squirt guns for an impromptu water fight. Everyone should let their inner child out now and again, right?

2 cups fresh peas

1 English cucumber, sliced

2 cups grape tomatoes, halved

2 teaspoons salt, or to taste

Freshly ground black pepper

⅓ cup olive oil

2 teaspoons apple cider vinegar

2 teaspoons balsamic vinegar

2 teaspoons minced garlic

2 teaspoons granulated sugar

2 teaspoons chopped fresh dill

1 dash red pepper flakes

Combine peas, cucumbers, and tomatoes in a large bowl. Sprinkle with the salt and pepper and refrigerate 20 minutes.

In a small bowl, whisk together the oil, vinegars, and garlic. Add the sugar and whisk to combine.

Pour everything over the veggies and sprinkle with dill and pepper flakes. Serve immediately or cover and serve within the hour. The cucumbers will start to pickle if you wait too long.

Serves 6.

GREEK SALAD

It is our dream to one day visit Greece and do absolutely nothing but wander the streets, stay up late to watch the moon and stars, and eat a lot of fresh food. Until then we've been creating our own Greek-inspired dishes from home and teaching the kiddos about dreams, goals, and visiting new countries. This Greek salad is fresh, easy, and refreshing on those hot summer nights.

1 English cucumber, chopped

2 cups grape tomatoes, sliced

½ red onion, sliced

½ cup sliced Kalamata or black olives

½ cup feta cheese crumbles

¼ cup olive oil

1 lemon, juiced

2 teaspoons vinegar

1 teaspoon granulated sugar

1 clove garlic, minced

1 teaspoon chopped fresh oregano

Salt and pepper to taste

In a large bowl, combine cucumbers, tomatoes, onion, olives, and feta cheese.

Whisk together remaining ingredients in a small bowl, pour over, salad, and toss to coast.

Chill until serving.

Serves 6.

WATERMELON SALAD

Watermelon is our girls' most favorite thing about summer (umm, what about strawberry shortcake?), so we try to find new ways to surprise them with it whenever we can. This salad is simple and refreshing, but make sure you use white balsamic vinegar. It's just barely lighter in flavor and goes nicely with the summer fruits.

5 cups chopped watermelon

2 cups sliced grape tomatoes

2 cups sliced red grapes

1 to 2 tablespoons olive oil

1 to 3 tablespoons white balsamic vinegar

Sea salt

1 tablespoon fresh chopped mint

1 tablespoon fresh chopped basil

TIP: Regular balsamic vinegar can be used if you can't find white balsamic, but try to go lighter.

Combine watermelon, tomatoes, and grapes in a large bowl. Chill 30 minutes in the refrigerator.

Drizzle chilled fruit with olive oil and vinegar to taste.

Sprinkle with salt, mint, and basil. Serve.

Serves 6 to 8.

BERRIES AND GREENS SALAD WITH POMEGRANATE-RASPBERRY DRESSING AND LEMON BROWN-SUGAR ALMONDS

This is our family's favorite salad because it's a perfect mashup of our entire family. Fruit and cucumbers for the girls, that slightly sweet and mildly salty cheese for Carrian, and the asparagus for Cade. And, oh, the peas! All of us love heading out to the garden and munching on fresh peas. Throw this salad together with a bright and springy pomegranate dressing, and it's the perfect go-to dish for BBQ's, potlucks, and get-togethers.

½ bunch (about 8 ounces) asparagus, woody ends cut off

Extra virgin olive oil

2 tablespoons garlic seasoning with parsley

1 (10-ounce) clamshell power greens

½ cup frozen peas, steamed and cooled

1 cup chopped cucumbers

1 cup grape tomatoes, chopped

1 cup sliced grapes

1 cup raspberries

1 cup sliced strawberries

½ cup cubed Dubliner cheese

1 batch Lemon Brown Sugar Almonds

Pomegranate-Raspberry Dressing

Heat a grill pan to medium high.

Place asparagus in a small bowl, drizzle with olive oil, and sprinkle with garlic seasoning. Toss to coat. Grill asparagus until char marks appear and stalks are tender. Remove from grill, cool, and chop into 1½-inch pieces; set aside.

In a large bowl, toss together greens, veggies, fruits, cheese, and asparagus.

Serve with Lemon Brown-Sugar Almonds and Pomegranate-Raspberry Dressing.

Serves 6 to 8.

POMEGRANATE-RASPBERRY DRESSING

½ cup canola oil

¼ teaspoon lemon zest

½ cup pomegranate juice

½ cup lemon juice

⅓ cup raspberries

⅛ teaspoon ground ginger

Pinch salt

Place all of the ingredients in a blender and pulse until smooth. Store in an airtight container in the refrigerator up to one week.

LEMON BROWN-SUGAR ALMONDS

¼ cup brown sugar

1 teaspoon lemon zest

½ cup slivered almonds

2 tablespoons butter

Line a baking sheet or cutting board with a sheet of parchment paper.

In a small bowl, stir together brown sugar and lemon zest; set aside.

Heat a small skillet over medium heat, add almonds, and toast, stirring occasionally, until almonds give off a nutty smell and begin to turn golden.

Add butter, and stir until melted.

Stir in the brown sugar–lemon mixture and toss to coat all the almonds.

Pour out onto parchment paper, spread out mixture, and let cool. Break apart any pieces and serve with your favorite salads.

side dishes

CILANTRO PESTO ASPARAGUS

Most people don't often think of cilantro and pesto together, but we've really enjoyed this new version of the old Italian classic. We tossed some leftover cilantro pesto over some asparagus and discovered a wonderful new flavor—bright, fresh, and a cinch to throw together.

¼ cup pine nuts

3 cups chopped cilantro

¼ cup olive oil

1 teaspoon lemon zest, plus more for garnishing

1 tablespoon lemon juice

2 cloves garlic, minced

¼ cup grated Pecorino Romano cheese

Salt and pepper to taste

1 pound asparagus, trimmed

Grated Parmesan cheese, for garnishing

Toast the pine nuts in a skillet over medium heat until golden, shaking pan or stirring nuts occasionally so they toast evenly. Remove from heat and set aside to cool.

In a blender or food processor, add the cilantro, pine nuts, olive oil, 1 teaspoon lemon zest, lemon juice, and garlic. Pulse until a thick paste forms.

Stir in the Pecorino cheese and season with salt and pepper to taste.

To store, pour into an airtight container and drizzle a little olive oil over the top. Press a piece of plastic wrap down against the pesto and cover with lid. Store in the refrigerator for up to 1 day. Bring to room temperature and stir well before serving.

To prepare asparagus: toss trimmed spears with salt and pepper to taste. Brush a grill pan with olive oil and heat over medium-high heat. Layer trimmed and seasoned asparagus in pan and cook until grill marks appear, rolling the spears to turn them.

Remove asparagus to a large serving plate and spoon Cilantro Pesto over top. Garnish with extra lemon zest and grated Parmesan.

Serves 4.

BROCCOLI WITH CHEESE SAUCE

Every recipe has a story, and this one is no different. Cade writes, "In college, I invited Carrian over for dinner one night. I wanted to impress her, so I went all out with steaks, potatoes, rolls, and this cheesy broccoli. It wasn't until we were engaged that she admitted she really didn't like broccoli until she had mine. She's been sold on it ever since."

1¾ cups shredded sharp cheddar cheese

2½ teaspoons cornstarch

3 cups broccoli florets

1 tablespoon salt, plus more to taste

¾ cup evaporated milk

Pinch dry ground mustard

Freshly ground black pepper

In a large bowl, toss shredded cheese with cornstarch and set aside to rest 10 minutes.

Meanwhile, bring a large pot of water to boil over medium-high heat.

Once water is boiling, add the 1 tablespoon salt and the broccoli. Cook no longer than 2 minutes. The broccoli should still be bright green and crisp tender. Remove broccoli with a slotted spoon and set aside in a large bowl.

In a medium saucepan over low heat, combine the cheese, milk, salt to taste, and ground mustard. Whisk until the cheese begins to melt.

Once melting beings, whisk occasionally until sauce reaches a low, soft boil. At this point, begin stirring constantly until slightly thickened, about 2 minutes.

Plate the reserved broccoli and spoon a generous amount of sauce over the broccoli. Top with fresh ground black pepper and serve.

Serves 4.

CANDIED PECAN BRUSSELS SPROUTS

Carrian never wanted anything to do with brussels sprouts until a new restaurant in town served them with bacon. We didn't know what the green was, but we dived right in, and by the last few bites kept eyeing the plate, wanting more but not wanting to be rude. When we learned the delicious dish was brussels sprouts, we both about fell out of our chairs and have been enjoying them ever since. This version is salty, sweet, crunchy, and a little buttery. The perfect homecooked dish with a twist.

3 slices bacon, cooked crisp and crumbled

2 cups trimmed and halved brussels sprouts

Olive oil

1 tablespoon unsalted butter

1 tablespoon garlic seasoning with parsley

⅓ cup Craisins

Candied Pecans

Heat pan to medium heat and add bacon. Cook until browned on either side and remove to a plate lined with paper towels. Cool. Crumble and set aside. Drain grease from pan, preserving remaining bacon bits in pan.

Heat a drizzle of olive oil and the butter in a sauté pan over medium heat.

Add brussels sprouts and stir to coat in the oil mixture. Sauté 5 to 10 minutes or until tender and golden on the cut side.

Stir in garlic seasoning with parsley and cook 1 more minute.

Remove to a serving dish and toss with Craisins, bacon crumbles, and Candied Pecans.

Serves 4.

CANDIED PECANS

3 cups roughly chopped pecans

1 egg white

2 teaspoons water

½ cup granulated sugar

½ cup brown sugar

1 tablespoon ground cinnamon

1 pinch ground nutmeg

1 pinch salt

Preheat the oven to 300 degrees F. and line a rimmed baking sheet with parchment paper.

Place pecans in a large bowl and set aside.

In a small bowl, whisk together the egg white and water until foamy. Stir into the pecans, followed by sugars, cinnamon, nutmeg, and a pinch of salt.

Spread coated pecans over prepared baking sheet and bake 25 to 27 minutes. Remove from oven and cool on counter several hours. Store in an airtight container.

HONEY ROASTED CARROTS

Carrian often tackles the main dish, and Cade makes the sides for dinner. (The kids set the table, and so far, no broken dishes!) These roasted carrots become sweeter when paired with butter and mustard.

1¼ **pounds baby spring carrots**

3 **tablespoons butter, melted**

2½ **tablespoons honey**

2½ **teaspoons dry ground mustard**

1 **teaspoon salt**

¼ **teaspoon ground black pepper**

Preheat oven to 400 degrees F.

In a large bowl, whisk together the butter, honey, mustard, salt, and pepper.

Toss in the carrots and stir to combine.

Spread everything on a rimmed baking sheet and bake 20 minutes, or until golden and tender.

Serves 2 to 4.

CREAMED CORN

Creamed corn is a classic Southern dish, so of course Cade grew up eating it. Carrian did too, though her creamed corn was from a can. Since "fresh is best," Cade challenged Carrian to make the best creamed corn ever. Though the corn is left whole in this recipe, the flavor of this one beat out all the rest. It is pure creamy deliciousness and made it easy to ditch the canned version.

4 cups frozen corn

3 tablespoons butter

1 tablespoon all-purpose flour

1 ounce cream cheese

1½ cups heavy cream

2 teaspoons all-purpose sugar

1 teaspoon salt (or to taste)

½ to ¾ cup shredded Colby Jack cheese

3 slices bacon, cooked crisp and crumbled

Pepper to taste

Melt butter in a medium saucepan over medium heat.

When butter starts to foam, whisk in the flour for 20 seconds and then, while still whisking, add the cream cheese and stir until the mixture all clumps together.

Whisk in the heavy cream. Add the sugar, salt, and cheese.

When mixture is very smooth, add the corn. Reduce heat to low and cook until corn is warmed through, stirring occasionally.

Season to taste and serve with crumbled bacon on top!

Serves 4 to 6.

FRESH GREEN BEAN CASSEROLE
WITH MATCHSTICK POTATOES

Carrian writes, "I love that Cade and I can be from different sides of the country, have grown up with different traditions, and yet be so completely compatible. For our first Thanksgiving together, I made the traditional green bean casserole, but as we ate I could tell Cade was thinking what I was thinking: This isn't as good as I remember. So we reinvented this classic with a cream of mushroom sauce and potatoes instead of onion on top. We don't make this casserole any other way now; it's that good!"

3 tablespoons unsalted butter

¼ cup minced onion

1 clove garlic, minced

½ cup minced white button mushrooms

3 tablespoons all-purpose flour

¾ cup heavy cream

½ cup chicken broth

Salt to taste

¼ teaspoon freshly ground black pepper

1 pound French green beans, washed and trimmed

1½ cups shredded Colby Jack cheese

Matchstick Potatoes

Preheat oven to 350 degrees F.

Melt the butter in a large saucepan over medium heat. Add the onion and garlic and sauté until tender, about 5 minutes. Add the mushrooms and sauté an additional minute.

Add flour and whisk 30 seconds to cook out the flour taste. Add cream and broth and whisk continuously until thickened, about 2 to 3 minutes.

Remove from heat and season with salt and pepper.

Add green beans and sauce mixture to a 9x9-inch casserole and stir to coat beans.

Top with shredded cheese and matchstick potatoes. Bake 30 minutes, until bubbly and heated through.

Serves 4 to 6.

MATCHSTICK POTATOES

1 large or 2 small russet potatoes, roughly peeled

¼ cup canola oil

Salt to taste

Using a mandolin set at the thinnest position, slice the potatoes.

Once sliced, stack several slices on top of each other and slice from top to bottom to make slices about the width of a matchstick or shoestring. Repeat until all potatoes have been sliced. Place sliced potatoes in a bowl of ice water.

Heat canola oil in a medium saucepan over medium-high heat until almost smoking. Drain the potatoes and pat dry with paper towels. Add potatoes and fry until golden, about 3 to 5 minutes.

Remove from oil with a slotted spoon and rest on a paper towel-lined plate to drain off excess oil. Sprinkle lightly with salt.

TWICE-BAKED SWEET POTATOES
WITH CRUMBLE TOPPING

Cade always requests these twice-baked sweet potatoes for Thanksgiving dinner, but they are perfect for any day of the year. He loves this mashup of sweet potato soufflé and twice-baked potatoes. And sometimes we add marshmallows under the topping. Just sayin'.

3 medium sweet potatoes

1 egg

2 tablespoons skim milk

½ teaspoon ground cinnamon

¼ cup (½ stick) butter, melted

Pinch salt

¼ cup granulated sugar

¼ cup brown sugar

Crumble Topping

Preheat oven to 350 degrees F.

Place the sweet potatoes on a baking sheet and, using a steak knife, carefully pierce each potato three times. Bake 1 hour, or until tender. Remove from the oven and allow to cool 30 minutes.

Slice each sweet potato in half lengthwise and carefully remove most of the insides, leaving a small amount lining the bottom. (This will help the skins hold their shape.)

Place the meat of each potato in a large bowl and add egg, milk, cinnamon, melted butter, salt, and sugars. Using a hand mixer, blend until thoroughly incorporated.

Spoon the mixture back into potato shells, creating a mounded look.

Spoon Crumble Topping over each potato and bake an additional 45 minutes.

Serves 4 to 6.

CRUMBLE TOPPING

½ cup brown sugar

½ teaspoon ground cinnamon

½ cup all-purpose flour

¼ cup (½ stick) butter, chilled and cubed

½ cup panko bread crumbs

In a small bowl, combine the sugar, cinnamon, and flour.

Using a pastry cutter or two forks, cut the butter into the mixture until it resembles wet sand.

Add the panko bread crumbs and mix to combine. Mixture should stick together when you grab it and press it together in the palm of your hand.

HONEY-MUSTARD ROASTED RED POTATOES

Carrian's family is from Oregon and Idaho, so russet potatoes were used in a lot of dishes. But over the years, we've discovered that different potatoes are meant for different dishes. Red and gold potatoes are creamier than their starchy russet cousin, and they are so good roasted with a Southern-inspired honey-mustard glaze!

1 pound red potatoes

2 to 3 tablespoons butter, melted

2 tablespoons honey

1 teaspoon dry ground mustard

½ teaspoon salt

¼ teaspoon black ground pepper

Preheat oven to 375 degrees F. and coat a baking sheet with nonstick cooking spray.

Scrub potatoes and cut in half or quarters, depending on the size. Layer cut potatoes on the prepared baking sheet.

In a small bowl, combine the butter, honey, mustard, salt, and pepper and then drizzle over the potatoes.

Bake 30 to 40 minutes, or until tender.

Serves 4.

LEMON GREEK POTATOES

Oh, sweet mercy, we love these perfectly roasted Lemon Greek Potatoes! One of the best tips we've learned for roasting potatoes is that a little broth or water keeps the potatoes from drying out and almost adds a little caramelizing action to the taters. Add a little fresh lemon, garlic, and plenty of salt, and you're in for a new favorite potato dish!

5 unpeeled russet potatoes, cut in wedges

1½ tablespoons sea salt or kosher salt

¾ cup water or chicken broth

Zest of 1 lemon

Juice of 1 lemon

¼ cup olive oil

3 cloves garlic, minced

2 teaspoons chopped fresh oregano

Preheat oven to 425 degrees F. and coat a baking sheet with nonstick cooking spray.

In a large bowl, toss the potatoes with salt and set aside.

In a small bowl, whisk together the water or broth, zest, lemon juice, oil, and garlic; pour over the salted potatoes.

Toss potatoes again and sprinkle with the oregano.

Layer potatoes on prepared pan and bake 1 hour and 20 minutes, stirring the potatoes every 20 minutes. If the liquid evaporates completely, add another ¼ cup. Serve hot!

Serves 6.

HEIRLOOM TOMATO TART

What is it about puff pastry that makes everything look so fancy? Its flaky shards of buttery goodness? That golden puff? We don't know, but we do know that one day we had a sheet of puff pastry that needed to be used and so we threw on a little tomato, mozzarella, and balsamic reduction and then our eyes proceeded to roll back in our heads out of pure delight. We eat this tart as an appetizer or even a main dish sometimes. It's fancy enough for guests and easy enough for a quick bite to eat.

1 cup balsamic vinegar

1 (17.3-ounce) package frozen puff pastry sheets

1 to 2 cups baby heirloom tomatoes, sliced in half

1 (8-ounce) tub marinated mozzarella pearls, marinade reserved

Preheat oven to 400 degrees F. and line a baking sheet with parchment paper.

In a small saucepan over medium-high heat, bring the balsamic vinegar to a boil and simmer until reduced by ½, about 35 minutes.

Meanwhile, unfold pastry sheets, stack on top of each other, and shape or roll into a rectangle. Slice stack in half lengthwise and transfer each stack to prepared baking sheet.

Using a sharp knife, carefully score a border around each puff pastry tart, about ¼- to ½-inch from the edges. Do not cut all the way through the dough. Bake 12 to 15 minutes, or until golden.

Remove puff pastry from the oven and lightly press down the middle to make it flat and even.

Once the balsamic vinegar is reduced, remove from heat and allow to thicken slightly as it cools.

Spread chopped tomatoes and the mozzarella pearls, along with some of their reserved marinade, over the middle of each puff pastry. Drizzle liberally with reduced balsamic glaze and serve.

Serves 4 to 6.

TIP: If serving as an appetizer, cut into squares or small circles for individual tarts.

CHEESY BASIL VEGGIES

Carrian writes, "In college, Cade and I were lucky enough to be friends with two of the sweetest people ever. Nic has since passed away, but since many of my first grown-up cooking days started with food shared with him and Cortney, we wanted to include a nod to our dear friends by celebrating these cheesy vegetables, which we first enjoyed in their home. They reminded me that food fresh from the garden is always a joy, and now Cade and I make this dish every summer."

2 medium carrots, peeled and sliced

2 small zucchini, sliced

2 small yellow squash, sliced

2 cloves garlic, minced

¾ cup shredded mozzarella cheese, divided

¾ cup grated Parmesan cheese, divided

¼ cup chopped fresh basil, plus extra for garnish

Salt and pepper to taste

¼ cup extra virgin olive oil

Preheat oven to 400 degrees F.

In a large bowl, combine all of the sliced vegetables.

Stir in the garlic, ½ cup of the shredded mozzarella, ½ cup of the grated Parmesan, the basil, and salt and pepper to taste.

Drizzle olive oil over vegetables.

Pour mixture into a 9x13-inch pan and bake 20 to 30 min, or until the vegetables are tender and the cheese is browning and bubbly.

During the last 10 minutes of cooking, top with remaining cheese. Garnish with a few basil leaves before serving.

Serves 4 to 6.

ROASTED ROOT VEGETABLES

Cade writes, "I love coming home to Carrian and the smell of something baking in the oven. When I walk through the door and those warm aromas hit me in the face, well, it's like I've just won a million bucks. Roasted root vegetables are one of my favorites because they are easy to make and they always taste like home—warm, comforting, with a flavor that fills your whole soul. Sometimes we add chicken breasts, cubed, and serve this as a main dish."

2 tablespoons olive oil, divided

1 large sweet potato, peeled and chopped

1 russet potato, peeled and chopped

4 small Yukon gold potatoes, chopped

2 cups chopped carrots

1 yellow onion, chopped

1 tablespoon kosher salt

½ teaspoon dried rosemary

½ teaspoon dried oregano

1 teaspoon dried basil

1 teaspoon parsley flakes

¼ teaspoon dried dill weed

2 cloves garlic, minced

2 teaspoons freshly squeezed lemon juice

Preheat oven to 400 degrees F.

Drizzle a rimmed baking sheet with 1 tablespoon of the oil to coat.

Add the veggies and remaining oil.

Sprinkle with all of the seasonings and garlic and toss to coat well.

Bake 35 to 45 minutes or until golden and tender. Sprinkle with lemon juice and serve immediately.

Serves 4.

TIP: Root vegetables—especially potatoes—love salt. Normally a sprinkle will do, but when roots are involved, add a little extra and keep taste-testing once cooked. Trust us, salt will elevate the whole dish.

BROWN-SUGAR GRILLED PINEAPPLE

Cade loves anything made on a grill—especially these juicy grilled pineapple slices slathered in a brown sugar butter sauce.

1 pineapple, peeled, cored, and sliced

6 tablespoons unsalted butter, melted

¾ cup brown sugar

Preheat grill pan to medium-high heat.

In a small bowl, combine the hot, melted butter with the brown sugar and stir until sugar is absorbed, about 1 minute.

Place pineapple slices on grill and cook until grill marks begin to appear. Flip and cook again on the other side, about 1 minute.

Remove pineapple slices from the grill and quickly brush the butter-brown sugar mixture over each side. Serve immediately.

Serves 4.

CILANTRO LIME QUINOA

Cilantro lime rice is delicious, but we've taken a lighter approach with a quinoa substitution. This side dish is healthy, filling, and a perfect accompaniment to nearly any main dish.

2 cups quinoa, rinsed

4 cups water

2 tablespoons unsalted butter

2 teaspoons chicken bouillon

1 handful chopped cilantro

Zest and juice from ½ a lime

1 (4-ounce) can diced green chiles

Combine all ingredients in a large saucepan over medium-high heat and bring to a rolling boil.

Cover with lid, reduce heat to low, and cook 15 minutes, or until quinoa is almost tender and liquid is absorbed.

Move pan off burner and let rest an additional 5 minutes or until tender.

Remove the lid, fluff with a fork to combine all ingredients, and serve immediately.

Serves 6 to 8.

FRIED RICE

The secret to making this faux takeout fried rice in your own kitchen is actually something Cade usually hates—leftovers! Just make rice one day and leave the leftovers in the fridge overnight. The drier rice will soak up all of the yummy sauce for the best fried rice ever.

3 cups frozen peas and carrots

2 eggs, beaten

2 tablespoons oil, divided

⅓ cup soy sauce

1 tablespoon brown sugar

½ teaspoon granulated sugar

⅛ teaspoon ground ginger

1 pinch crushed red pepper flakes

4 cups cooked rice

2 cups chopped, cooked ham

2 green onions, chopped, for garnish

1 teaspoon sesame seeds, for garnish

Steam the peas and carrots and set aside.

Add 1 teaspoon oil to a small skillet and heat over medium heat. When oil starts to shimmer, pour in beaten eggs and begin lifting and tilting the pan to distribute the egg evenly and completely over the bottom of the pan. Cook for a minute or two and then carefully flip and cook until set. Remove the egg, chop, and set aside.

In a small bowl, whisk together the soy sauce, sugars, ginger, and crushed red pepper. Set aside.

Heat remaining oil in a large sauté pan over medium heat until the oil is shimmering. Add rice and sauté until it is hot and begins to pop.

Stir in the sauce mixture to combine. Add the eggs, ham, carrots, and peas and stir until heated through.

Top with green onion and serve immediately.

Serves 6 to 8.

MEXICAN FRIED RICE

When we were in our college cooking class together, we learned to make a bacon fried rice, which quickly became one of our favorite dishes to make together. And since fried rice is best made with day-old (or two-day or three-day old) rice, this was the perfect solution for poor college students on a budget. Now we like to invent new fried rice recipes or mashups, like this Mexican version.

3 teaspoons canola oil, divided

1 red bell pepper, chopped

1 yellow bell pepper, chopped

½ onion, chopped

2 eggs, beaten

4 to 5 cups Mexican Rice, prepared and refrigerated at least 1 day in advance (see recipe below)

2 tablespoons Worcestershire sauce

1½ tablespoons granulated sugar

1 teaspoon lime juice

Dash Tabasco

Heat 1 teaspoon oil in a skillet over medium heat. Add peppers and onion and sauté, stirring occasionally, 5 to 10 minutes or until tender. Remove to a plate and set aside.

Add 1 teaspoon oil to the same skillet and heat until oil begins to shimmer. Pour in beaten eggs and begin lifting and tilting the pan to distribute the egg evenly and completely over the bottom of the pan. Cook for a minute or two and then carefully flip and cook until set. Remove the egg, chop, and set aside.

Heat remaining teaspoon oil in the same skillet. When oil begins to shimmer, add cold Mexican Rice and stir until heated through.

In a small bowl, stir together the Worcestershire, sugar, and lime juice. Add to the rice, stirring to coat evenly. Add the peppers, onion and egg back in and toss to combine.

Serve immediately.

Serves 6 to 8.

MEXICAN RICE

1½ cups rice, preferably Calrose rice

1½ cups chicken broth

1½ cups water

1 (10-ounce) can Rotel diced tomatoes with cilantro and lime juice

¼ cup chopped fresh cilantro

1 clove garlic, minced

Dash salt

Add rice, chicken broth, water, tomatoes, cilantro, garlic, and salt to a large pot and bring to a rolling boil over high heat.

Cover, reduce heat to low, and cook about 20 minutes, until liquid is absorbed and rice is tender.

Remove from heat and allow to cool completely before storing in an airtight container in the refrigerator for up to 3 days.

ORANGE CRANBERRY RICE PILAF

Carrian would rather vacuum the whole house than think up a side dish for dinner, but then we created this orange cranberry rice pilaf. It is delicious because it has a little bit of everything—citrus, fresh herbs, sweet Craisins, and starchy rice. Plus the presentation is beautiful, which is great for when company is coming.

2 tablespoons butter

1 shallot, minced

1 small clove garlic, minced

Zest of 1 orange

½ cup Craisins

1 cup plus 2 tablespoons orange juice, divided

Pinch salt

¼ teaspoon ground cinnamon

¼ cup granulated sugar

2 cups rice

3 cups chicken stock or broth

⅓ cup sliced almonds

¼ cup chopped fresh parsley, for garnish

Melt butter in a large, nonstick skillet over medium heat. When butter begins to foam, add the shallots and cook until tender, stirring occasionally.

Add the garlic, orange zest, Craisins, 2 tablespoons of the orange juice, salt, cinnamon, and sugar and cook, stirring, for 1 minute.

Add rice and cook another 3 minutes, stirring occasionally, until rice turns translucent.

Transfer rice mixture to a large saucepan; add remaining 1 cup orange juice and the chicken broth. Bring to a rolling boil over medium-high heat. Once boiling, cover with lid, reduce heat, and cook 20 minutes, or until rice is tender and liquid is absorbed.

Meanwhile, toast the almonds, stirring occasionally, in a nonstick skillet over medium-low heat until just starting to turn golden in color, about 3 to 5 minutes. Set aside.

Once the rice is cooked, fluff with a fork, toss with toasted almonds, and sprinkle with parsley for a garnish.

Serves 6 to 8.

ROASTED RED PEPPER MAC 'N CHEESE

This is just about the creamiest, cheesiest pasta ever, and it has a secret: roasted red peppers! Cade says macaroni and cheese is a recipe every Southern family has mastered, but this recipes puts a fresh spin on it. You won't know the pureed peppers are in there until that extra layer of flavor hits your taste buds.

1 pound small shell pasta

3 roasted red bell peppers

½ cup (1 stick) unsalted butter

1 clove garlic, minced

½ cup all-purpose flour

1 cup milk

1 cup heavy cream

1 cup finely shredded medium cheddar cheese

1 cup finely shredded mild cheddar cheese

Pinch ground nutmeg

1¼ teaspoons kosher salt

¼ teaspoon ground black pepper

Prepare pasta according to package directions in boiling, salted water. Drain, reserving about ¼ cup of the liquid, and set aside.

Place roasted red peppers in a blender jar and puree until smooth; set aside. (To roast your own bell peppers, simply heat a gas burner on your stovetop and use long-handled tongs to hold a pepper over the flame, turning as needed, until skin is wilted and blackened. Alternatively, you can steam the peppers in a plastic bag and remove the skin after a few minutes.)

Melt butter in a large pot over medium heat until butter begins to foam. Add the garlic and sauté until fragrant, 20 to 30 seconds.

Quickly whisk in the flour, cooking about 30 seconds.

Whisk in the pureed roasted red pepper until well combined. Continue to whisk while gradually adding milk and cream.

Whisk until smooth and then add cheeses, nutmeg, salt, and pepper. Whisk until all of the cheese is incorporated; shredding the cheese using the smallest holes on a box grater will produce a creamier sauce.

Spoon the pasta into the mixture, adding a tablespoon or two of the reserved pasta water if needed to thin the sauce. Serve immediately.

Serves 4 to 6.

POTATO ROLLS

Every cook claims to make the fluffiest, squishiest, best-gosh-darn rolls ever, but they would be wrong. Big time. This recipe is the best ever.

3 cups milk

¾ cup granulated sugar

¾ cup (1½ sticks) unsalted butter

1 cup potato flakes

1 tablespoon salt

1 tablespoon instant yeast

4 eggs, lightly beaten

7 cups all-purpose flour, divided

⅓ cup butter, softened

In a medium saucepan over medium heat, heat milk until almost simmering, but do not allow it to boil. (Scalded milk makes rolls super light and fluffy.) The edges will begin to foam and froth, and a thin film may appear on top of the milk (gently lift off film if it does appear).

Remove scalded milk from heat and stir in the sugar, butter, potato flakes, and salt. Combine well and then allow to cool to lukewarm.

Add the yeast, stir, and then add the eggs, stirring until they are mixed in.

Place 5 cups of flour in a large bowl. Pour the milk mixture in and stir until the dough has come together but is still soft. Add up to 2 cups flour, as needed. Dough will be slightly sticky.

Cover the bowl with a clean tea towel or plastic wrap. Let dough rise 1 hour. (If preparing dough in advance, cover dough and refrigerate overnight. Then return to room temperature and continue with baking directions.)

When dough has risen and is ready to shape, gently push it down, and then divide it into 4 equal parts.

Preheat oven to 350 degrees F. and lightly grease 2 baking sheets.

On a lightly floured surface, roll 1 portion of dough into a circle. Spread softened butter over the dough and then roll out another circle. Place on top, gently pressing together. Cut the dough into wedges and, starting with the wide end, gently roll dough to the tip. Place on prepared baking sheet.

Repeat until all dough is used. Cover baking sheets with a clean tea towel and let rise 1 to 2 hours, or until doubled in size.

Bake rolls 14 to 20 minutes, until golden brown, checking frequently during final few minutes of baking.

Makes about 32 rolls, depending on size.

SWEET POTATO ROLLS

Since Cade is obsessed with sweet potatoes, we had no choice but to experiment until we found the best sweet potato roll variation. Yes, the rolls will look slightly orange, which we find kind of beautiful, but the flavor is amazing, and these babies are soft and fluffy.

⅔ cup milk

5 tablespoons unsalted butter, diced

3 tablespoons granulated sugar

1 teaspoon dry active yeast

2¾ cups bread flour

1½ teaspoons kosher salt (or ¾ teaspoon sea salt)

1 teaspoon vital wheat gluten

1 sweet potato, baked, skin removed, and mashed (1 cup)

1 large egg with 1½ teapoons egg white removed

Butter for tops after baking

In a large glass measuring cup, heat milk in the microwave on high power for 90 seconds.

Remove from microwave, add diced butter, and stir until butter is melted.

Once mixture is warm but not hot, add the sugar and yeast and set aside.

In the bowl of a stand mixer equipped with the paddle attachment, add the flour and salt. On the side of the bowl opposite the salt, add the vital wheat gluten and mix on low.

Add the yeast mixture, mashed sweet potato, and egg. Mix again just until the dough comes together and then switch to the dough hook and mix for 90 seconds.

Drape a light towel or plastic wrap over the bowl and allow dough to rise 1 to 2 hours.

Sprinkle the counter lightly with flour and turn out the very soft dough. Sprinkle the top of the dough with a little more flour and roll out into a ¼-inch thick rectangle. Starting at the end closest to you, tightly roll the dough into a log. Cut dough into 2-inch pieces and use the palm of your hand to gently roll each piece of dough in to a very round ball.

Place on a greased cookie sheet, cover with a clean towel, and allow to rise 1 to 2 hours, until doubled in size.

Heat the oven to 350 degrees F. and bake 18 to 20 minutes

Quickly brush the tops with more butter and serve warm.

Makes 16 to 20 rolls.

TIP: Vital wheat gluten can be found in the baking section of your grocery store. It can be omitted if needed.

TIP: To easily remove 1½ teaspoons of egg white, place in bowl and whisk slightly.

FRESH GARDEN SALSA

We love fresh chips and salsa as a side or appetizer—or even a late-night snack—and this is by far our favorite salsa recipe. The secret is to use a variety of tomatoes and let the fresh flavors do all the talking. We like a mix of red, yellow, sunburst, and baby heirloom purple tomatoes.

2 to 3 cups chopped baby heirloom tomatoes

Juice of 1 lime

2 small cloves garlic, minced

⅓ cup minced onion

⅓ cup chopped cilantro

Dash red pepper flakes

1 teaspoon cumin

Salt and pepper to taste

In a small bowl, toss the tomatoes, lime juice, garlic, onion, cilantro, red pepper flakes, and cumin together. Allow to sit for at least 30 minutes.

Drain off most of the juices and season to taste with salt and pepper.

Serves 4.

FRUIT SALSA WITH CINNAMON-SUGAR CHIPS

Fresh fruit plus cinnamon-sugar fried tortilla chips equals pure deliciousness. It doesn't matter if it's an appetizer, snack, side dish, or even dessert, Carrian sets the bowl in front of her and refuses to share. Though, to be fair, we all it love it just as much as she does, and when we see those chips start coming out of the fryer, we all go crazy. They are awesome!

2 peaches, chopped

2 nectarines, chopped

4 kiwi, peeled and chopped

1 mango, peeled and chopped

2 (16-ounce) packages strawberries, chopped

1 tablespoon lemon juice

¼ cup strawberry jam

6 uncooked tortillas

2 tablespoons unsalted butter, melted

½ cup cinnamon sugar

Add all of the fruit to a large bowl, drizzle with lemon juice and jam, and lightly fold everything together. Store in the refrigerator until ready to serve. (Don't refrigerate longer than 3 hours or the juices will begin to break down the fruit.)

Preheat oven to 400 degrees F. and line a rimmed baking sheet with parchment paper. Set aside.

In a skillet over medium heat, cook the tortillas one at a time according to package directions. Brush each cooked tortilla with melted butter and then sprinkle with cinnamon sugar.

Use a pizza cutter to slice tortillas into triangles and then arrange on prepared baking sheet.

Bake 5 to 8 minutes, until chips are crispy. Serve with chilled Fruit Salsa!

Serves 6 to 8.

main dishes

GARDEN SKILLET

We love summer cooking because everything is so fresh and accessible. We especially love dishes that can be made with or without meat. We're trying to maintain a healthy weight, so we mix things up during the week. Some nights are vegetarian, others meat, and some nights we enjoy a little dessert after dinner. It's all about balance. And this dish has great balance, so you can use whatever is bursting from the garden.

6 turkey meatballs, cooked and chopped (optional)

Olive oil

1 small to medium zucchini, chopped

Salt and pepper to taste

¾ cup sugar sweet or sunshine tomatoes

¾ cup grape or cherry tomatoes

1 heirloom tomato, chopped

⅓ cup marinara sauce

¾ cup shredded mozzarella cheese

Fresh chopped basil

Heat a drizzle of olive oil in a large skillet over medium heat. Add the zucchini and sprinkle with salt and pepper to taste. Sauté 1 minute.

Add the meatballs, if using, the tomatoes, and sauce. Cook until the tomatoes are bursting, zucchini is tender, and everything is hot.

Sprinkle with cheese, cover with lid, and cook 1 to 2 minutes more, until cheese melts.

Serve with fresh basil and more salt and pepper if needed.

Serves 4.

EASY SAUSAGE ALFREDO

Our #1 dream travel destination is Italy. Oh, the food! When we were first married, we would snuggle up on the couch and watch Everyday Italian *on the Food Network and then create our own versions of classics. We took a regular creamy chicken alfredo recipe and gave it a new twist with sausage, sun-dried tomatoes, and bright peas to add a little pop!*

4 garlic sausages

½ cup water

¼ cup (½ stick) unsalted butter

2 cloves garlic, minced

1 tablespoon all-purpose flour

4 ounces cream cheese, chopped in cubes

1 cup heavy cream

⅔ cup grated Parmesan cheese

Salt and pepper to taste

½ pound penne pasta

¾ cup frozen peas, defrosted in a bowl of warm water.

1 cup oil-packed sun dried tomatoes, drained

¼ cup fresh chopped parsley

Cook the sausages in a large skillet over medium heat for 6 to 8 minutes, turning often. Add ½ cup water and place a lid over the pan. Continue to cook 10 to 15 minutes or until cooked through. Remove the sausages to a cutting board and tent with foil. After a few minutes, slice sausages diagonally and recover with foil.

Melt the butter in a large skillet over medium heat. Add the garlic, stirring a few times, and cook 30 seconds. Quickly whisk in the flour and cook, stirring continuously, for 30 seconds.

Add the cream cheese to the pan and stir until the cream cheese starts to melt down a little. Pour in the cream and Parmesan and cook, whisking continuously, until the cream cheese is incorporated. Tiny pieces of cream cheese might not melt all the way but should once the pasta is added and the heat is reduced. Once the sauce has thickened, season with salt and pepper to taste.

Meanwhile, cook the pasta to al dente according to package directions. Using a spider or slotted spoon, scoop the pasta into the sauce and add the sausage, peas, and tomatoes. If the sauce is too thick, add a little of the pasta water, a tablespoon at a time. Stir everything together and garnish with parsley.

Serves 4.

ZUCCHINI LASAGNA

Ricotta cheese is our go-to favorite cheese for this lasagna, but when we were looking to make a lighter version of this classic dish, we tried it with cottage cheese, which goes nicely with the zucchini. Speaking of which, start off by sautéing or grilling your zucchini and then pat it dry, otherwise you'll end up with too much water in the dish. And for a quick vegetarian version, simply omit the ground beef.

6 zucchini, sliced lengthwise

1 pound ground beef (a 60/40 mix works best)

1 tablespoon butter

1 teaspoon olive oil

½ cup minced onion

1 red bell pepper, minced

1 yellow bell pepper, minced

1 large clove garlic, minced

1 (6-ounce) can tomato paste

2 (15-ounce) cans tomato sauce

1 (15-ounce) can good quality diced tomatoes

2 teaspoons fresh chopped basil

2 teaspoons dry Italian seasoning

3 shakes red pepper flakes

Salt and pepper to taste

1 heaping cup cottage cheese

4 cups shredded mozzarella cheese

6 teaspoons grated Parmesan cheese

Preheat oven to 375 degrees F.

Heat a grill or grill pan to medium heat. Grill the zucchini on each side for a minute or two and remove to a plate. After zucchini has rested for a few minutes, place a colander over a large bowl, line with a paper towel, and place zucchini in the colander to allow excess liquid to drain off and prevent zucchini from being mushy. Pat slices dry and set aside.

Heat butter and oil in a large pot over medium heat. If using beef, add ground beef and cook while stirring occasionally, until almost brown; add onion, peppers, and garlic and cook until tender, about 2 minutes.

Stir in tomato paste, sauce, and diced tomatoes. Add basil, Italian seasoning, red pepper flakes, and salt and pepper to taste. Stir to combine and allow to simmer 10 minutes. Remove from the heat.

Assemble lasagna: Spoon ½ cup of the sauce over the bottom of a 9x13-inch baking pan. Line the pan with drained ⅓ of the zucchini slices and top with a heaping ⅓ cup cottage cheese, using the back of a spoon to spread it out. Carefully spread ¾ cup of the sauce over the cottage cheese, sprinkle with 1 cup shredded mozzarella, and 2 teaspoons grated Parmesan cheese. Repeat the layers 2 more times, ending with sauce and the 2 cheeses.

Cover lasagna with aluminum foil that has been sprayed with cooking spray to prevent sticking and bake 30 minutes. Remove the foil and bake an additional 10 minutes, or until cheese starts to turn golden.

Let lasagna rest outside oven 5 to 10 minutes before serving.

Serves 8 to 10.

CHICKEN CORDON BLEU LASAGNA

We love making classics from scratch and mashing them up, like with this chicken cordon bleu lasagna. The secret to its amazing taste is the nutmeg in the sauce. Add a little nutmeg to any white sauce, and your family will be begging for more. To make preparations just a little bit easier, we recommend using a store-bought rotisserie chicken.

7 tablespoons unsalted butter, divided

1 tablespoon minced garlic

¼ cup all-purpose flour

1 cup heavy cream

2½ cups milk

½ teaspoon salt

1 bay leaf

½ teaspoon ground nutmeg

¼ teaspoon ground black pepper

¾ cup grated Pecorino Romano cheese, divided

2⅓ cups shredded Swiss cheese, divided

⅔ cup panko bread crumbs

1 (9-ounce) box oven-ready lasagna noodles (12 noodles)

3 cups cooked and shredded chicken

2 cups chopped, cooked ham

1½ cups shredded mozzarella

Parsley for garnish

Preheat oven to 400 degrees F. Coat a 9x13-inch baking pan with non-stick cooking spray.

Melt 5 tablespoons butter in a large Dutch oven over medium heat. Once butter is melted and starts to foam, add the garlic and cook, stirring occasionally, for 1 minute. Whisk in the flour and cook 1 to 2 minutes until nutty and fragrant but not brown. Whisk in the cream and milk. Add the salt, bay leaf, and nutmeg and simmer 10 minutes.

Stir in ½ cup of the pecorino Romano and ⅓ cup of the Swiss cheese and cook an additional 5 minutes. Remove from the heat.

Melt remaining 2 tablespoons butter in a nonstick skillet over medium heat. Once melted, add the bread crumbs and stir occasionally until lightly golden, about 1 to 2 minutes. Set aside.

To assemble lasagna: Spoon ⅓ cup of the sauce over the bottom of the prepared baking dish. Use 4 lasagna noodles to cover the bottom of the dish. Spoon ⅔ cup sauce on top of the noodles, followed by half of the chicken and ham, ½ cup of the shredded Swiss cheese, and a pinch of the pecorino Romano. Repeat with another set of 4 noodles, ⅔ cup sauce, the rest of the chicken and ham, ½ cup shredded Swiss cheese, and another pinch pecorino Romano. Finish by layering 4 more noodles, the rest of the sauce, and the remaining cheese, this time including the mozzarella.

Cover pan with a sheet of aluminum foil sprayed with nonstick cooking spray and bake 20 minutes. Remove the foil, top with buttered bread crumbs, and bake an additional 20 minutes until the cheese is gooey and noodles are soft. Let rest 10 minutes before serving.

Serves 8 to 10.

BRAISED DIJON CHICKEN AND POTATOES

This skillet dinner is our #1 favorite recipe. Sure, there are others that come in at a very close second, but we've yet to beat this combination of sweet caramelized onions, roasted potatoes, and juicy chicken. And don't even get us started on the sauce!

5 bone-in chicken thighs

1 teaspoon kosher salt

Ground black pepper

⅓ cup apple cider vinegar

¼ cup Dijon mustard

2 cloves garlic, minced

¼ cup granulated sugar

½ teaspoon smoked paprika

6 slices bacon

2 tablespoons unsalted butter

1 small yellow onion, chopped

6 to 8 small Yukon gold potatoes, quartered

1¼ cups chicken broth

1 tablespoon fresh chopped parsley

Preheat oven to 450 degrees F.

Season chicken thighs with salt and pepper and set aside.

In a small bowl, whisk together the vinegar, mustard, garlic, sugar, and paprika. Set aside.

Cook bacon in a heavy, cast-iron skillet (or an oven-safe nonstick skillet) over medium heat until crisp, turning to ensure even crisping. Remove the bacon to a paper-towel lined plate and drain off all but 1 tablespoon of the grease in the pan. Chop the bacon and set aside.

Return skillet with 1 tablespoon of the bacon fat to the stove and heat over medium high. Add the chicken, skin side down, and reduce heat to medium-low. Cook 3 to 5 minutes, or until the skin is golden brown; flip and continue cooking another 5 minutes on the other side. Remove the chicken to a plate.

Increase heat to medium and add 2 tablespoons butter to the pan. Once butter has melted, add the onion and sauté 2 to 3 minutes. Add the potatoes and sauté 4 to 5 minutes.

Nestle the chicken, including any juices that have collected on the plate, back in the skillet. Add the reserved vinegar mixture and broth.

Simmer for 1 minute and transfer pan to preheated oven for 35 to 40 minutes. The juices will thicken up, and the chicken will stay moist due to the liquid. Remove from the oven and sprinkle with chopped bacon and parsley. Serve with pan juices spooned over the top of the chicken and potatoes.

Serves 4 to 6.

TIP: If using boneless, skinless chicken breasts or thighs, reduce baking time to 15 to 20 minutes.

COCONUT CHICKEN CURRY

As a family, we like to try new things like soccer for the girls, or traveling to new places, or making new friends. We also like to be adventurous with our flavors. We've started a tradition of learning about different countries online and then trying a recipe from those countries. Coconut chicken curry is a super mild and creamy dish and is one of our current favorites.

2 to 4 skewers

2 boneless, skinless chicken breasts

Pinch salt and pepper

2 tablespoons curry powder, divided

1 tablespoon garam marsala, divided

1 medium yellow onion, diced

2 cloves garlic, smashed

1 (14-ounce) can sweetened coconut milk, full fat

2 tablespoons tomato paste

1 teaspoon salt

Ground black pepper, to taste

1 teaspoon granulated sugar

2 tablespoons water

1½ tablespoons cornstarch

2 cups cooked white rice for serving

Cilantro for garnishing

Chop the chicken into large chunks. Sprinkle with a little salt and pepper, half of the curry, and half of the garam masala. Toss to coat evenly. Thread the chicken onto skewers. (If you are using wooden skewers, soak them in water for an hour before threading the chicken.)

Heat a grill or grill pan to medium-high. Add skewered chicken. Turn the chicken every 1 to 2 minutes until grilled on each side, about 6 to 8 minutes total. Set aside.

Heat the oil in a large skillet over medium heat until shimmering. Add the remaining curry and garam marsala. Cook, stirring occasionally, for 1 minute.

Add the onion and a little more oil if the pan is dry. Sauté 2 to 3 minutes, or until the onion is tender, stirring often. Add the garlic and cook an additional 30 seconds.

Stir in coconut milk, tomato paste, salt, pepper, and sugar.

In a small bowl, whisk together the water and cornstarch and then whisk into the sauce.

Simmer 15 minutes.

Add grilled chicken pieces, stir to combine, and heat 3 minutes.

Serve topped with fresh cilantro over cooked white rice.

Serves 4.

TIP: To make a vegetarian version, substitute 1 sweet potato, 1 can of chickpeas (drained), and 1 small white potato instead of chicken.

FIESTA CHICKEN AND RICE

This recipe is a fiesta in your mouth! It's everything you could want in a dish—a fresh squeeze of lime, a sprinkling of cilantro, and some mild avocado to cut the spice—all served in one pan for a family-style dinner. Feel free to use white or brown rice, or even quinoa!

4 teaspoons chili powder

2½ teaspoons salt, divided

2¼ teaspoons smoked paprika

2 teaspoons granulated sugar

1 teaspoon onion powder

1 teaspoon garlic powder

¼ teaspoon cayenne pepper

1¼ teaspoon cumin

3 boneless, skinless chicken breasts

1 tablespoon cornstarch

2 tablespoons canola oil, divided

1 cup brown rice

1 cup chicken broth

1 cup water

1½ tablespoons freshly squeezed lime juice

1 (4-ounce) can diced green chiles

1 (15-ounce) can black beans, drained

1½ cups frozen corn

¾ cup shredded Mexican cheese blend

2 tomatoes, chopped

Avocado

Cilantro, for garnish

In a small bowl, stir together chili powder, 2 teaspoons salt, smoked paprika, sugar, onion powder, garlic powder, cayenne, and cumin.

To a large Ziploc bag, add the chicken breasts, cornstarch, and 2 tablespoons of the seasoning. Seal the bag and shake to coat the chicken.

Heat 1 tablespoon oil in a large, deep skillet over high heat until it begins to shimmer. Add the chicken and reduce heat to low. Cook 6 to 7 minutes, flip over, and continue cooking until cooked through, about 4 to 6 minutes.

Remove the chicken to a plate and tent with foil.

Place the skillet back on the burner over medium heat. Add the remaining oil and the rice. Cook, stirring occasionally, for 2 minutes to toast the rice. Add the broth, water, remaining seasoning, lime juice, remaining salt, and diced green chiles. Bring mixture to a boil, reduce heat to low, place the lid on the skillet, and cook 45 minutes for brown rice, or 20 to 30 minutes for white rice.

Remove the lid, add the beans, corn, cheese, and tomatoes. Season to taste, and stir. Arrange the chicken on top and cover with lid. Let mixture simmer 10 minutes to bring all ingredients to the same temperature.

Chop chicken into bite-sized pieces and serve with fresh avocado slices and cilantro.

Serves 4.

TERIYAKI CHICKEN AND RICE CASSEROLE

This casserole is a yummy mashup of one of our faux takeout favorites. (Really, it's just a fancier version of our Fried Rice recipe with a killer teriyaki sauce.) Feel free to double the recipe to serve a large family gathering or bring to a potluck. It's the perfect recipe to showcase farm-fresh veggies like broccoli, sprouts, carrots, or snow peas.

3 cups Fried Rice (see recipe on page 86)

¾ cup low-sodium soy sauce

½ cup water

⅓ cup brown sugar

1 tablespoon honey

¾ teaspoon ground ginger

1 teaspoon sesame oil

1 small clove garlic, minced fine

2 tablespoons cornstarch

2 tablespoons cold water

1 large chicken breast

1 small package stir-fry vegetables including broccoli, sprouts, carrots, and snow peas, found in the produce section of the grocery store

Prepare Fried Rice as directed on page 86.

Preheat oven to 350 degrees F.

In a medium saucepan, stir together the soy sauce, water, brown sugar, honey, ground ginger, sesame oil, and garlic. Bring to a boil and cook for 1 minute.

In a small bowl, stir together the water and cornstarch. Add 1 teaspoon of the hot soy sauce mixture to the cornstarch mixture and then slowly pour everything into the boiling soy sauce mixture, whisking until it begins to thicken. Set aside.

Place the chicken in a baking dish and pour 1 cup of the teriyaki sauce over the chicken. Bake 30 minutes, remove from the oven, and shred.

Steam the veggies and then add the veggies, rice, and shredded chicken to an 8x8-inch baking dish. Add 3 tablespoons of the leftover teriyaki sauce and stir to combine. Place the dish back in the oven for 15 minutes, remove from the oven, and drizzle with a little more sauce. Serve immediately.

Serves 4.

GREEK CITRUS CHICKEN

Here are three helpful tips that will make cooking chicken in a pan a breeze. First, set out your chicken 5 minutes before cooking. Cold meat doesn't cook through evenly. Second, start with high heat and add your chicken, then turn to low—that will provide color and allows for even cooking. When the meat has turned white halfway up the breast, flip it and cook the other side until no pink remains.

4 boneless, skinless chicken breasts

⅓ cup olive oil

1⅓ cups orange juice, divided

1 tablespoon Greek seasoning

2 teaspoons salt

Pinch ground black pepper

2 cloves garlic, minced

¾ cup oil packed sun-dried tomatoes, drained

To a large Ziploc bag, add the chicken, olive oil, ⅓ cup of the orange juice, and seasonings. Seal tightly and squeeze the bag all over to coat the chicken. Refrigerate 2 hours or up to overnight.

Heat an oiled grill pan over high heat.

Remove the chicken from the Ziploc bags and discard the marinade.

Place the chicken on the hot grill and reduce the heat to medium-low. Cook 6 to 7 minutes on one side. Turn the chicken and cook an additional 6 to 7 minutes or until cooked through (temperature on a meat thermometer should read 165 degrees F.). Remove chicken to a serving platter and tent with aluminum foil to keep it warm.

In a small saucepan over medium heat, bring the remaining orange juice and sun-dried tomatoes to a simmer. Simmer 2 minutes.

Remove foil from chicken and pour sauce over top. Return to skillet, spooning sauce over top of chicken. Cook 1 minute. Remove to serving dish and rest 2 to 3 minutes.

Serves 4.

GREEK SEASONING

1 tablespoon dried oregano

2 teaspoons dried thyme

2 teaspoons dried basil

1½ teaspoons dried rosemary

2 teaspoons dried dill

2¼ teaspoons dried parsley

2 teaspoons onion powder

2½ teaspoons garlic powder

2 teaspoons salt

1 teaspoon ground black pepper

½ teaspoon marjoram

½ teaspoon ground cinnamon

¼ teaspoon nutmeg

Combine all ingredients in a medium bowl.

Transfer to a mason jar, screw on the lid, and store up to 6 months with your other spices.

DOUBLE-THE-MEAT, HOLD-THE-BREAD BLT WITH CILANTRO-LIME DRESSING

This salad is like a protein overload, and, good mercy, it's incredible. The marinated meats are juicy and flavorful, and the crisp, salty, slow-cooked bacon gives it a mouth-watering crunch, but the star of the show is the bright cilantro lime dressing. Pile it up with fresh greens, creamy avocado, and juicy grape tomatoes and you've got yourself a show-stopping salad.

2 cloves of garlic, minced

1½ tablespoons Montreal chicken seasoning

3 tablespoons Worcestershire sauce

3 tablespoons red wine vinegar

¼ cup plus 1 teaspoon olive oil

1 (2-pound) flank steak

4 boneless, skinless chicken breasts, pounded flat or butterflied

1 (8-ounce) bag baby spinach

1 (8-ounce) bag baby arugula or watercress

Olive oil

1 lemon, juiced

6 slices bacon, cooked and crumbled

2 cups grape tomatoes, sliced

1 avocado, chopped

Cilantro-Lime Dressing

In a medium bowl, whisk together garlic, Montreal chicken seasoning, Worcestershire sauce, and red wine vinegar. Slowly add the oil while whisking continuously.

Divide the marinade between two Ziploc bags. Place the chicken in one bag, and the steak in the other. Seal well and marinate from 15 minutes to overnight.

Remove steak and chicken to separate plates and discard marinade. On a grill or grill pan heated to medium, cook chicken 6 to 7 minutes and steak 8 to 9 minutes. Flip chicken and steak and allow the chicken to cook an additional 3 minutes and the steak an additional 5 to 7 minutes. (For chicken, 165 degrees F. on a meat thermometer; for steak, 140 to 145 degrees F.) Remove meat to a clean cutting board and tent with aluminum foil. This will allow the juices to redistribute for better tasting meat. After 5 minutes, slice thin on the diagonal and set aside.

To serve family style, place some spinach and arugula on a large platter and lightly drizzle with a little olive oil and the juice from 1 lemon. Stack the steak, chicken, and bacon on top, followed by the tomatoes and avocados. Drizzle with the Cilantro-Lime Dressing and serve immediately.

Serves 6 to 8.

CILANTRO-LIME DRESSING

1 bunch cilantro, stems cut off

3 cloves garlic, minced

9 limes, juiced

½ cup apple cider vinegar

½ cup rice vinegar

⅓ cup granulated sugar

¾ teaspoon salt

½ cup canola oil

1 medium to large tomatillo, peeled

Place all ingredients in the jar of a blender and process until smooth. Store in refrigerator 7 to 9 days.

SMOKY SLOPPY JOES

Carrian writes, "Cade and I were married for almost ten years before I knew that he liked sloppy joes. I hated them when I was younger and never thought to try them as an adult. But when Cade mentioned that he really enjoyed sloppy joes, I immediately started testing recipes. I'd try one, then he'd try one, and finally we threw in a little butter and liquid smoke and bam! We were in love."

3 tablespoons butter

½ cup finely diced onion

1 red bell pepper, chopped

1½ teaspoons garlic, minced

1 pound ground beef (an 80/20 mix works best)

2½ tablespoons brown sugar

2 tablespoons Dijon mustard

2 tablespoons Worcestershire sauce

¾ teaspoon liquid smoke

1 tablespoon chili powder

1 teaspoon smoked paprika

1 cup ketchup

¼ cup apple cider vinegar

Salt and pepper to taste

Buns for serving

TIP: For less vinegar flavor, start with 1 to 2 tablespoons and add more as desired.

Melt butter in a large Dutch oven over medium heat. Add the onion and sauté until translucent, about 5 minutes. Add the peppers and garlic and stir occasionally for 1 minute.

Add the ground beef and break it up with a wooden spoon, stirring it all together. Allow to cook for 3 minutes, stirring occasionally.

Add the brown sugar, mustard, Worcestershire, liquid smoke, chili powder, and paprika. Stir for 30 seconds and then add the ketchup and vinegar. Allow to cook 5 minutes, season to taste, and serve or simmer up to 1 hour on low and then serve. The longer it cooks the better the flavor.

Scoop onto buns that have been brushed with butter.

Serves 4.

BUSY DAY CASSEROLE

This casserole takes forever to cook, but on a busy day, dinner can take care of itself in the oven so we don't have to stand over the stove with a million pots. It was Carrian's favorite meal as a kid, though her mom made it with condensed soup. And, though the recipe calls for ground beef, you can also make it with cooked, shredded, or chopped chicken. It also is the perfect dish to add more veggies like broccoli, peas, or corn.

3 tablespoons unsalted butter

¼ cup minced onion

1 garlic clove, minced

½ cup minced white button mushrooms

3 tablespoons all-purpose flour

½ cup heavy cream

½ cup chicken broth

¼ teaspoon freshly ground black pepper

Salt to taste

1 cup long grain white rice

2 cups water

½ to 1 pound cooked ground beef

1 cup sliced carrots

9 slices cheddar or Colby Jack cheese

Preheat oven to 350 degrees F. and coat a 9x9-inch baking dish with non-stick cooking spray.

Melt the butter in a medium saucepan over medium heat. Whisk in the onion, garlic, and mushrooms and sauté several minutes.

Add the flour, whisking continuously, and cook 30 to 60 seconds. Add the cream and broth and cook until thick and bubbly. Season with pepper and salt to taste and remove from heat.

Combine white sauce, rice, water, cooked ground beef, and carrots in prepared baking dish and bake 90 minutes.

Top with the cheese and bake for a few more minutes or until melted.

Serves 4 to 6.

SWEET AND SOUR MEATBALLS

We learned how to make this sweet-and-sour sauce for egg rolls in a cooking class we took together. It has such a fantastic flavor that we are always looking for new ways to use it. This recipe mashup can be baked in the oven as directed or in a slow cooker set on low for 3 to 4 hours. If you want to lighten it up, just use ground turkey in place of the ground beef.

2 pounds ground beef (an 85/15 mix works best)

⅔ cup panko bread crumbs

2 tablespoons dry minced onion

1 large egg

¼ cup coconut milk

1½ teaspoons ground ginger

2 teaspoons salt

¼ teaspoon ground black pepper

1 tablespoon canola oil

⅓ cup chopped red bell pepper

⅓ cup chopped yellow bell pepper

⅓ cup chopped green bell pepper

1 clove garlic, minced fine

1½ teaspoons onion powder

½ cup rice vinegar

½ cup ketchup

¼ cup low-sodium soy sauce

2 cups granulated sugar

⅛ teaspoon sesame oil

½ (11-ounce) can mandarin oranges, smashed with their juices

2 to 3 tablespoons cornstarch

¼ cup cold water

Sesame seeds for garnish

Green onions for garnish

Rice for serving

Preheat oven to 400 degrees F. Grease a 9x13-inch baking pan. Or if using a slow cooker, lightly oil the cooking insert.

To a large bowl, add ground beef, bread crumbs, onion, egg, coconut milk, ginger, salt, and pepper. Mix with your hands until just combined. Rub a little oil on your hands and then roll the meat mixture into 1-inch balls. Place meatballs in prepared baking pan or slow cooker.

Bake 20 minutes in the oven or set slow cooker to low and bake, covered with sauce, 3 to 4 hours.

To make the sauce: In a saucepan over medium heat, add the oil, chopped peppers and garlic. Sauté until tender, about 3 minutes. Add onion powder, vinegar, ketchup, soy sauce, sugar, and sesame oil. Stir to combine and then add the oranges and juice. Bring to a boil.

Meanwhile, stir the cornstarch and water together and then whisk into the sauce. Bring back to a boil, then reduce heat to medium-low and simmer 10 minutes. Serve over meatballs with sesame seeds and green onions to garnish.

Serves 6.

STEAK BURRITOS WITH GRILLED ZUCCHINI

We love to combine fresh ingredients with strong flavors. This burrito is stuffed with grilled veggies like zucchini and corn, fresh salsa, and marinated meat that's got a little caramelization from the grill . . . and then, oh, sweet mercy, that smoky sauce!

Look for Cotija cheese and the crema Mexicana cheese in fresh Mexican section of the store or by the meat section by the fresh tortillas and salsa. You could also substitute queso fresco or Monterey Jack cheese, if you choose.

Tortillas

1 (1- to 2-pound) flank steak

Salt

Pepper

Cumin

1 zucchini, sliced in half lengthwise and drizzled with olive oil, salt, and pepper

2 ears corn on the cob

1 cup crumbled Cotija cheese

1 cup fresh salsa

⅓ cup crema Mexicana

1 teaspoon chili powder

¼ teaspoon smoked paprika

Juice from ½ lime, about 1 tablespoon

Lime wedges for garnishing

¼ cup chopped cilantro

Heat a griddle to medium heat and cook the tortillas on each side until they begin to brown and bubble; set aside.

Place the meat on a platter and sprinkle evenly on each side with salt, pepper, and cumin to taste.

Cover a grill on high heat until it is nice and hot.

Remove lid or cover from grill and reduce heat to medium-high. Place the meat on the grill and close the lid. Cook 6 to 9 minutes and then flip over. Add zucchini and corn to the grill. Cook the vegetables 2 to 3 minutes, until grill marks appear, and flip to the other side. Cook the meat another 6 to 9 minutes.

Remove meat and vegetables from the grill to a cutting board, and tent with foil; let the meat rest 5 to 8 minutes.

Meanwhile, place the crema Mexicana, chili powder, and lime juice in a bowl and whisk until everything is well incorporated; set aside.

Slice the corn off of the cob and chop the zucchini into chunks.

Slice the meat into thin strips.

Place a dollop of the crema mixture on a tortilla, followed by steak, zucchini, corn, salsa, Cotija crumbles, cilantro, and a squeeze of lime. Fold in the top and bottom of the burrito; then grab a side, pull it up over the filling, and tuck it under the filling, continuing to roll the burrito shut. Serve immediately.

Serves 4.

TIP: Because flank steak is usually tapered, one end will cook faster than the other. Simply cut steak in half and cook separately. Cook thinner end 4 to 6 minutes.

CAROLINA PULLED PORK WITH SAUCE

Any real Southerner knows that the best pulled pork cooks low and slow. And since this dish must be started 2 days ahead of serving, it clearly is the best recipe ever. Don't worry, though, it really doesn't take much work, and most of the time is so the pork can soak in a brine before being slipped into the oven. And, oh, the wait is so worth it! Just remember that it is as important to let the meat rest as it is to cook it slow, so don't skip that step.

1 (5- to 8-pound) pork shoulder or butt roast, bone in and fat pad on top

4 cups water

4 cups apple cider

½ cup kosher salt

½ cup dark brown sugar

Dry Pork Rub (see recipe on page 128)

1 pinch red pepper flakes

2 bay leaves

Carolina Vinegar Sauce (optional) (see recipe on page 128)

Mustard BBQ Sauce (optional) (see recipe on page 128)

Two days before serving, combine the water, apple cider, salt, sugar, 3 heaping tablespoons of the Dry Pork Rub, pepper flakes, and bay leaves in a large stockpot. Rinse off the pork and place it in the pot, making sure it is completely covered by the brine. Lid the pot and place it in the refrigerator 12 to 24 hours.

The day before serving, preheat the oven to 225 degrees F.

Remove the pork from the brine and place in a roasting pan or 9x13-inch baking pan, fat pad up. Make sure the sides of the roast do not touch the sides of the pan. Pat roast very dry with paper towels. Remove 2 tablespoons of the Dry Pork Rub to a small Ziploc bag and set aside for later use. With your hands, rub the remaining Dry Pork Rub all over the pork and in any cracks or flaps.

Return roast, fat-side facing up, to the pan, insert an oven thermometer in the thickest part of the meat, and roast 12 to 14 hours, until the thermometer registers 200 degrees F. Some ovens turn off automatically after 12 hours, so make sure to check yours and turn it back on if needed.

When the temperature reaches 200 degrees F., turn off the oven and leave the pork in there to rest 2 hours. If you need the oven for other purposes, remove the pan, cover the meat with foil, and allow it to rest on the counter for 2 hours.

Once the meat has rested, remove the fat from the top. Drain off and reserve half of the pan juices. In a large bowl or dish, using two forks, shred the meat and remove the bone. Pour some or all of the reserved pan juices and the reserved Dry Pork Rub to taste over the meat and toss to coat. Serve as is or on buns with either Carolina Vinegar Sauce or Mustard BBQ Sauce drizzled over everything.

Serves 12.

DRY PORK RUB

1 tablespoon onion powder

1 heaping tablespoon smoked
  paprika

1 tablespoon garlic powder

1 tablespoon chili powder

1½ tablespoons kosher salt

1 tablespoon pepper

2 teaspoons cayenne powder

2 teaspoons dry mustard

1 tablespoon cumin

½ cup dark brown sugar

Combine all ingredients in a medium bowl and transfer to a mason jar. Screw lid on tightly and store until ready to use, or up to 2 months.

CAROLINA VINEGAR SAUCE

½ cup apple cider vinegar

½ cup white vinegar

¼ to ½ cup brown sugar

½ teaspoon chili powder

2 pinches red pepper flakes

Salt to taste

Combine all ingredients in a small bowl and refrigerate until ready to use.

MUSTARD BBQ SAUCE

¾ cup yellow mustard

½ cup honey

¼ cup apple cider vinegar

2 tablespoons ketchup

1 tablespoon brown sugar

2 teaspoons Worcestershire sauce

1 teaspoon hot sauce, or to taste

2 tablespoons butter, melted

Pinch of nutmeg

Dash liquid smoke

Add all ingredients to a bowl and whisk to combine. Pour sauce into a jar with a lid and refrigerate for 1 day to 1 week prior to serving, as this builds the best flavor. Sauce can be refrigerated for up to 2 months.

BBQ PULLED PORK TACOS

It seems like everyone is obsessed with #tacotuesday, but since neither of us grew up eating tacos, we are always looking for ways to mashup taco recipes with a childhood favorite. Since BBQ is in Cade's blood, we wanted to make a southern taco with juicy pulled pork, thick slabs of bacon, with cool and crunchy coleslaw, all stuffed into crispy fried taco shells!

1 (3.5-pound) boneless pork butt roast

1 teaspoon fresh ground black pepper

1½ tablespoons kosher salt

1 teaspoon cayenne pepper

2 teaspoons smoked paprika

1 teaspoon garlic powder

1 teaspoon onion powder

1 teaspoon dried thyme

Corn tortillas

Canola oil for frying

10 slices bacon, cooked crisp and crumbled

Coleslaw, homemade or store-bought

Barbecue sauce

Cilantro for garnish

In a small bowl combine all of the seasonings.

Rub seasoning mixture generously over all sides of the pork and place in a slow cooker set on low for 8 hours.

When ready to assemble tacos, pour ½ inch oil in a large skillet over medium heat. When oil begins to shimmer, use tongs to place one tortilla at a time in the hot oil. Flip tortilla with tongs after 2 to 3 seconds in the oil and then gently fold up one, making sure it does not touch the other side of the tortilla. Cook for a few seconds and then flip and repeat to make a taco shell. Set shell upside down over a paper-towel lined plate (do not lay shell on its side). Continue until all tortillas have been fried and shaped into shells. Sprinkle with a little sea salt.

Fill each taco with pork, bacon crumbles, and coleslaw. Drizzle with barbecue sauce and top with cilantro.

Serves 4 to 6.

ASIAN STICKY SLOW COOKER RIBS WITH STICKY SAUCE

Carrian loves to cook everything she can get her hands on, but ribs are Cade's territory. Our favorites are baby back ribs because they end up fall-off-the-bone juicy. Make sure you have lots of napkins on hand when eating!

2 racks pork baby back ribs

½ cup light brown sugar

1 tablespoon smoked paprika

2 teaspoons chili powder

1 tablespoon garlic powder

½ teaspoon black ground pepper

Sticky Sauce

In a small dish, combine brown sugar, paprika, chili powder, garlic powder, and pepper.

Make sure the membrane has been removed from the underside of the ribs, then massage the dry rub onto both sides. Curl the ribs into the slow cooker, so they go around the sides. Pour half of the Sticky Sauce over the ribs; reserve other half of sauce in a small bowl for later use. Place the lid on the slow cooker and cook on low 6 to 8 hours.

Line a broiler pan with aluminum foil. Remove the ribs from the slow cooker and place them on the lined pan, meaty side up. Brush some of the reserved Sticky Sauce over the ribs and leave the rest for serving. Broil on high 2 to 3 minutes, until sauce looks sticky and bubbly and begins to char. Rest, tented with foil, 5 minutes before serving with Sticky Sauce.

Serves 4 to 6.

STICKY SAUCE

2 teaspoons ground ginger

2 teaspoons ground pepper

1 teaspoon onion powder

6 cloves garlic, minced

1 tablespoon sweet chili sauce (found in the international section of the grocery store)

⅔ cup reduced-sodium soy sauce

⅔ cup balsamic vinegar

⅔ cup brown sugar

⅔ cup honey

1 tablespoon cornstarch

1 tablespoon water

In a small bowl, whisk together the ginger, pepper, and onion powder. Add the garlic and mix again. Add the wet ingredients and whisk to combine.

Transfer sauce to a medium saucepan and bring to a boil over medium heat. Once sauce begins to boil, whisk the cornstarch and water together in a small dish and add 1 tablespoon of the hot liquid. Stir together and then, while whisking constantly, slowly drizzle cornstarch mixture back into the saucepan.

Whisk until sauce returns to a boil, reduce heat to medium-low, and simmer until it begins to reduce and thicken, anywhere from 1 to 10 minutes. Remove from the heat and set aside until ready to use.

TAILGATER NACHOS

These are not your typical nachos, but they are a perfect way to use leftovers from the Carolina Pulled Pork recipe. It's a mashup of Southern pork, potatoes from the Northwest, and a whole lot of cheese and bacon.

1 (1.5- to 2-pound) pork butt or shoulder roast

1 tablespoon salt plus more for seasoning potatoes

4 russet potatoes, cut in half and sliced thin

Olive oil

Shredded Colby Jack cheese

1 pound bacon, cooked crisp and crumbled

Sour cream

Barbecue sauce

Chopped cilantro

Sprinkle pork roast liberally with up to 1 tablespoon salt, place in slow cooker and cook on low 8 hours, until tender and falling apart.

Thirty minutes before serving, heat oven to 450 degrees F.

Drizzle a little olive oil on a cookie sheet and toss the sliced potatoes in the oil. Sprinkle a little salt on top and bake 10 to 15 minutes, flipping halfway, until golden and tender.

While potatoes bake, shred the pork.

Layer the potatoes, pork, cheese, and bacon in a cast-iron skillet or on a cookie sheet, finishing with cheese on top, and broil on high until melted and gooey.

Sprinkle additional bacon on top, along with sour cream, barbecue sauce, and cilantro as desired.

Serves 6.

GRILLED AVOCADO TACOS

This is one of those recipes that we would be willing to get on our knees and beg you to try. It's a simple list of ingredients and benefits from mixing it up with your own variations like grilled corn, spicy jalapeños, or even a little bacon, but no matter what you try, don't skip the lime—it's what makes the tacos unbeatable

5 corn tortillas

1 ripe but firm avocado

Salt and pepper

Olive oil

⅓ cup crumbled queso fresco

1 lime, cut in wedges

Heat a grill or grill pan to medium-high heat.

Cut open the avocado and remove the pit but not the peel at this point. Brush each open face with olive oil and sprinkle with salt and pepper. Place cut side down on the grill and cook 2 to 5 minutes or until grill marks have appeared. Remove from the grill and allow to cool while you proceed.

Place each tortilla on the grill and grill each side for a few seconds, flip, and cook again, until grill marks begin to form and the tortilla puffs slightly. Remove from the grill and set on a plate.

To assemble tacos, slice the avocado in ⅛-inch slices lengthwise, remove from the peel, and layer a few slices in each tortilla, along with a little cheese, a squirt or two of lime juice, and a pinch of salt.

Serves 2 to 3.

desserts

DEEP-FRIED STRAWBERRY SHORTCAKES

Even our kids know that Carrian's favorite dessert is strawberry shortcake. She waits all year for berry season just so she can try new versions. This one is a Southern-version of strawberry shortcake—in other words, it's deep-fried. Enough said.

1 (16.2-ounce) can refrigerated biscuits

Peanut or canola oil for frying

1 to 2 pints strawberries, sliced

1 to 2 tablespoons granulated sugar

¾ cup cinnamon sugar

2 cups heavy cream

½ cup powdered sugar, or to taste

Separate biscuits into 8 pieces and then split each piece in half to total 16 pieces; set aside.

Add enough oil to a Dutch oven or other heavy pot to fill it ⅓ full. Turn heat to medium.

While oil heats, toss strawberries with sugar in a small bowl and set aside. Add cinnamon sugar to a shallow bowl and set aside.

Test oil temperature by dipping the handle of a wooden spoon in the hot oil. If oil bubbles steadily, it's ready. If, however, it bubbles very, very rigorously, reduce heat and let it cool just a touch. Place 2 or 3 biscuits at a time in the hot oil and fry 30 to 60 seconds, turning once with long tongs. Remove to a paper-towel-lined plate to drain off excess oil.

While the biscuits are still warm, roll each of them in the cinnamon sugar.

In a large bowl with an electric mixer or the whisk attachment of a stand mixer, beat the cream until soft peaks form. Add the powdered sugar and beat until stiff peaks form.

To assemble shortcakes, top each fried biscuit with a spoonful of berries and a generous dollop of whipped cream. If desired, stack another biscuit on top and add more berries and cream for a double-decker shortcake.

Serves 8.

LEMON-STRAWBERRY SHORTCAKES

Cade might deep-fry his shortcakes, but Carrian loves them light and lemony. They look like regular short-cakes, but the light zip of the lemon brightens up the whole dish in an unexpected way. It's like summer in your mouth!

1 pint strawberries, sliced

½ cup plus 2 tablespoons granulated sugar, divided

2 cups all-purpose flour

1 tablespoon baking powder

¾ teaspoon kosher salt

Zest of 1 lemon

½ cup (1 stick) cold, unsalted butter, cut in small cubes

1 large egg, slightly beaten

1 tablespoon lemon juice

¼ cup heavy cream, plus a few tablespoons for topping

¼ cup whole milk

2 cups sweetened whipped cream

Toss strawberries with 2 tablespoons of the sugar in a medium bowl and refrigerate until ready to serve.

In a separate, medium bowl, whisk together 5 tablespoons of the sugar, the flour, baking powder, salt, and lemon zest.

With a pastry cutter or 2 knives, cut the cold butter into the flour mixture until it resembles small peas.

Add the slightly beaten egg, lemon juice, ¼ cup heavy cream, and milk to the dry ingredients and use a fork to gently mix.

Turn out dough on a lightly floured surface and gently knead until everything is holding together. Roll the dough out to ½-inch thick and use a glass or biscuit cutter to cut out shortcakes.

Place cut shortcakes on a baking sheet, wrap with plastic wrap, and let rest in the refrigerator 30 minutes.

Preheat oven to 425 degrees F.

Remove shortcakes from fridge, brush the tops with the remaining heavy cream, and sprinkle with remaining sugar. Bake 12 to 15 minutes.

Cool cakes, split them open (or use 2 per person), and top with prepared berries and whipped cream.

Serves 8.

PASTRY FOR SINGLE-CRUST PIE

This pastry is perfect for single-crust pies, such as Dutch apple, cream pies, and berry pies. Be sure to use very cold butter and chilled shortening when making. Using a stick of shortening makes it easy to chop it into pieces. If using shortening from a can, measure and add each tablespoon individually. Don't skip letting the finished dough chill in the refrigerator. The bits of cold butter and shortening in the dough are what help produce a flakier, more tender crust.

1⅓ cups all-purpose flour

½ teaspoon salt

2 tablespoons cold butter, cut into 4 pieces

6 tablespoons shortening, chilled and chopped

3 to 4 tablespoons ice water

Add flour and salt to the bowl of a food processor and pulse once or twice to combine.

Distribute butter pieces over the flour in the food processor and pulse a few times; distribute shortening pieces over mixture and pulse about 10 times until pea-sized pieces form and the mixture resembles coarse crumbs.

Transfer mixture to a medium bowl. Add 1 tablespoon ice water at a time, tossing carefully with a rubber spatula after each addition. Use enough of the water to make the dough just stick together when scooped up and shaped with clean hands.

Turn dough out onto a piece of plastic wrap and form into a disc about 1-inch thick. Don't worry if there are still crumbs around; just press them into the disc and wrap tightly with the plastic wrap. (If your dough is too wet, the crust will be tough.)

Refrigerate 30 minutes or up to several days if preparing in advance. If the recipe for which you are preparing the pastry dough calls for an unbaked pie crust, stop here and follow the directions in that recipe to finish your dish.

If your recipe calls for a prebaked or blind baked (partially baked) pie shell, preheat oven to 375 degrees F.

Remove dough from refrigerator. (If dough was chilled longer than 30 minutes, let it sit on the counter briefly before rolling it out.) Roll out chilled dough on a floured surface into an ⅛-inch thick round. To achieve a rounder circle, turn the dough over and rotate it a quarter circle after every two passes with the rolling pin.

Once dough is rolled out, fold one edge of the circle up over the rolling pin, as if you are going to wrap the dough around it. Carefully lift up the dough circle and drape it over a 9-inch pie plate. Gently press sides and bottom down to line the pie plate. Trim excess dough, leaving a ½- to ¾-inch overhang. Fold edges under and pinch or flute as desired.

Before baking, use the tines of a fork to press holes all over the bottom and sides of the dough. Alternatively, line dough with foil or parchment paper, leaving enough of an overhang to grab and lift off foil with both hands during baking. Pour pie weights or 2 to 3 cups dried beans over the foil to weigh it down. Either method will work to prevent bubbles from forming in the crust and stop the dough from shrinking.

Bake in preheated oven 25 to 30 minutes, until crust has turned a deep golden brown. If using pie weights, carefully lift out foil or parchment paper 15 to 20 minutes into baking and continue baking an additional 5 to 10 minutes until crust has turned a deep golden brown.

Remove from oven and cool on a wire rack before filling.

FOOLPROOF DOUBLE-CRUST PIE DOUGH

3 cups all-purpose flour

1 teaspoon salt

¼ cup butter, cut into pieces

¾ cup shortening, chilled in the fridge

½ cup very cold water

1 large egg

1 tablespoon vinegar

In a large bowl, whisk together flour and salt.

With a pastry cutter, 2 forks, or even your clean hands, cut the butter and shortening into the flour until it resembles pea-sized crumbs; set aside.

In a small bowl, whisk together the water, egg, and vinegar.

Make a well in the center of the flour mixture and slowly pour in liquid while using a fork to pull down the flour and mix as you pour. When the dough has come together but a little flour remains, stop adding the liquid. It's common to have some liquid left over.

Divide dough in half and form into 2 discs. Wrap in plastic wrap and chill in the refrigerator if using that day. Otherwise, store in the freezer up to 2 months.

DULCE DE LECHE BANANA CREAM PIE

Carrian writes, "My sister is quite a few years older than I am, so anytime we did something together when I was little, I felt incredibly special. On one occasion we stopped at a restaurant for banana cream pie but somehow had only a checkbook with us when the waiter came with our bill. The restaurant wouldn't accept checks. We were practically in tears and had to call our mom to come rescue us. Now, whenever I feel the need for banana cream pie, I just make this one at home. It's a delicious mashup of two of my favorite flavors."

1 (3.4-ounce) box French vanilla instant pudding

1 cup milk

4 ounces light cream cheese, softened

½ (14-ounce) can sweetened condensed milk

2 cups freshly whipped cream (make sure it is whipped to stiff peaks) or nondairy whipped topping

2 bananas, sliced

1 prepared graham cracker pie crust

1 (15-ounce) can Dulce de Leche

In a large bowl, whisk the pudding and milk together according to package directions and set aside.

In another bowl, with an electric mixer, beat the cream cheese until smooth, about 2 minutes, and then add the sweetened condensed milk; beat again.

Fold the pudding into the cream cheese mixture and stir until evenly combined.

Gently fold in ⅓ of the whipped cream. Add the remaining whipped cream and fold until completely combined.

Layer the sliced bananas on the bottom of the pie crust and cover with Dulce de Leche. This usually ends up being about ¾ of the can.

Spread the filling on top and chill before serving.

Serves 8.

DUTCH APPLE PIE WITH WHITE-CHOCOLATE BUTTER SAUCE

Cade makes a fantastic Southern apple pie, but we've added a brown-sugar streusel topping and White-Chocolate Butter Sauce for this version of the ultimate all-American dessert.

Pastry for Single Crust Pie, unbaked (see recipe on page 138)

3 honey crisp apples, peeled and sliced

3 granny smith apples, peeled and sliced

1 cup granulated sugar

1¼ cups plus 1½ teaspoons all-purpose flour, divided

⅛ teaspoon ground nutmeg

1 teaspoon ground cinnamon

Salt

1 cup plus 1 tablespoon all-purpose flour

1½ cups rolled oats

1½ cups brown sugar

¾ cup (1½ sticks) cold, unsalted butter

White-Chocolate Butter Sauce

Preheat oven to 375 degrees F.

Roll chilled, prepared pastry dough into a ⅛-inch thick circle and line a 9-inch pie plate with the dough; trim and crimp the edges, and then chill in refrigerator while preparing filling.

In a large saucepan over medium heat, add the apples, sugar, 3 tablespoons plus 1½ teaspoons of the flour, nutmeg, cinnamon, and a pinch of salt. Cook, stirring occasionally, 10 to 12 minutes or until slightly tender. Watch the apples carefully. You want them to still have a bite to them; don't let them get mushy.

Pour the apples into the unbaked pie shell.

In a small bowl, whisk together remaining 1 cup plus 1 tablespoon flour, oats, brown sugar, and a pinch of salt. Cut in butter with a fork or pastry cutter to make crumbs and then use your hands to finishing mixing until a sandy, crumbly topping forms.

Sprinkle crumbs over apples and bake pie 25 to 35 minutes or until golden and bubbling.

Serve with ice cream and drizzle with White-Chocolate Butter Sauce.

Serves 8.

WHITE-CHOCOLATE BUTTER SAUCE

¼ cup (½ stick) butter

¼ cup powdered sugar

2 tablespoons cream cheese

2 tablespoons white chocolate melts or almond bark

Using an electric mixer, beat together butter, powdered sugar, and cream cheese until smooth.

When ready to serve sauce, place butter mixture in a microwave-safe bowl and heat on high power 45 seconds.

In a separate small bowl, melt the white chocolate or almond bark in the microwave on high power in 30-second increments, stirring often. Once smooth and melted, stir into the warm butter mixture.

DEEP-FRIED PEACHES

Deep-fried peaches with ice cream, sticky caramel, and bright red berries—a little bit Southern with a farm-to-table twist. Snag yourself some sweet, tree-ripened peaches and dip them in a quick batter, then straight into the hot oil. Immediately roll in cinnamon sugar and pile on the toppings. It. Is. Heaven.

4 large peaches, unpeeled, sliced in half, pits removed

¾ cup cinnamon sugar, plus more for sprinkling on peaches

1 cup all-purpose flour

1 cup milk

1 tablespoon granulated sugar

1 large egg

¾ teaspoon baking powder

¼ teaspoon sea salt

Peanut oil

Vanilla ice cream

Fresh whipped cream

Fresh raspberries

Caramel sauce (optional)

Place the open peach halves on a cutting board and sprinkle with cinnamon sugar; let rest 30 minutes.

Meanwhile, place ¾ cup cinnamon sugar in a pie dish or shallow bowl; set aside.

In a medium bowl, whisk together the flour, milk, sugar, egg, baking powder, and sea salt until batter is smooth; set aside.

Fill a large pot ⅓ full of peanut oil, or enough to cover half a peach, and set over medium heat. Once the oil begins to pop and snap (drop a little water in or touch a wooden spoon handle to the bottom to test it), you are ready to go.

Add each peach half to the batter and coat evenly. Quickly lift out and let excess batter drip back into the bowl. Add peach halves to the hot oil and fry about 3 minutes, until batter is crisp and golden, turning occasionally. Watch carefully, as oil temperatures can vary widely and thus cook the peaches more quickly than 3 minutes.

Remove peaches with a slotted spoon and immediately drop in the reserved cinnamon sugar, turning to coat.

To serve, set peach halves in ice cream dishes, top with ice cream, whipped cream, a sprinkle of cinnamon sugar, caramel sauce, and fresh berries.

Serves 8.

RAZZLEBERRY CRISP

Carrian lived on crisps and cobblers while growing up in Washington, and her personal favorite was always made with marionberries. But when they aren't in season, a combination of blackberries and raspberries still makes a crisp you can't resist. A hint of Saigon cinnamon gives a little extra warmth, and a crumble topping adds the perfect finishing touch.

4 cups blackberries

4 cups raspberries, fresh or frozen

½ granny smith apple, grated

½ cup granulated sugar

1 cup plus 2 tablespoons all-purpose flour, divided

½ teaspoon Saigon cinnamon

1½ cups rolled oats

1½ cups brown sugar

¾ cup (1½ sticks) butter, unsalted

Pinch salt

Vanilla ice cream, for serving

Preheat oven to 350 degrees F.

In a large bowl, toss the berries and grated apple with the granulated sugar, 2 tablespoons of the flour, and cinnamon.

Pour berry mixture into 2 tart dishes or an 8x8-inch baking dish.

In a large bowl, combine the remaining 1 cup flour, oats, brown sugar, and salt and mix thoroughly.

Cut in the butter with a pastry cutter and then use your hands to gently squeeze and mix the topping until it all comes together when squeezed in the palm of your hand.

Bake 20 to 30 minutes, until golden on top. Serve warm with ice cream.

Serves to 4 to 6.

TIP: Saigon cinnamon tends to have a flavor superior to basic ground cinnamon. It's available in many supermarkets, and can even be found in bulk at Costco.

RASPBERRY LEMON TART BARS

We love to work in the kitchen together at night. After the kids go to bed, we take 30 minutes to create something amazing for the next day. One night we were making lemon curd, and Carrian dipped a raspberry in it for Cade. We ended up sitting at the counter dipping berry after berry in the pot until not a drop was left. Which led to this creation.

2 tablespoons buttermilk

2 large egg yolks

¾ teaspoon vanilla

2½ cups plus 3 tablespoons all-purpose flour, divided

1⅓ cups powdered sugar

Pinch salt

1 cup (2 sticks) cold, unsalted butter, cut in small cubes

1⅓ cups raspberries

1¾ cups granulated sugar, divided

4 large eggs, lightly whisked

3 tablespoons all-purpose flour

1 teaspoon lemon zest

⅔ cup freshly squeezed lemon juice

Prepare the crust: in a small bowl, whisk the buttermilk, egg yolks, and vanilla together with a fork; set aside.

To the bowl of a food processor, add 2½ cups flour, the powdered sugar, and salt and pulse to combine. Add the butter pieces and then pulse 10 to 12 times.

With food processor running, pour in the buttermilk–egg yolk mixture. Once the dough begins to come together, turn it out onto a sheet of plastic wrap and press into a disc. Wrap tightly in the plastic wrap. Chill in the refrigerator 1 hour or in the freezer 15 to 20 minutes.

Coat a 9x9-inch baking dish with nonstick cooking spray. Remove dough from refrigerator and press it evenly to all sides of the sprayed pan. Cover tightly with plastic wrap and freeze 20 minutes.

Preheat oven to 375 degrees F. Remove plastic wrap from the prepared pan and bake 20 to 25 minutes, until crust is no longer doughy but is not yet golden in color.

While crust bakes, gently fold together the raspberries and ¼ cup of the granulated sugar in a small bowl; set aside.

In a separate bowl, prepare the custard filling: whisk together the eggs, remaining 1½ cups granulated sugar, the remaining 3 tablespoons flour, and lemon zest until mixture is thick and pale yellow. Add the lemon juice and whisk until smooth.

Once the crust is baked, remove from oven and reduce temperature to 325 degrees F. Drain the juices from the berries into the custard filling and whisk to combine. Scatter the berries over the crust and then pour the custard over the berries.

Bake 20 to 30 minutes or until the center does not jiggle.

Remove from the oven and allow to cool completely. Serve once cool or cover with plastic wrap and serve the next day.

Serves 6 to 9.

KEY LIME BARS

These bars are a fun twist on key lime pie, a classic Southern dessert. This sweet-and-tart recipe can be easily halved and baked in an 8x8-inch pan if you want to make a smaller batch. For the full recipe, make sure you have enough graham crackers and limes on hand. Nine whole graham crackers typically yields 1 cup crumbs; 10 to 12 limes typically produces 1 cup juice.

3 cups crushed graham cracker crumbs

¾ cup (1½ sticks) unsalted butter, melted

¼ cup granulated sugar

Pinch salt

2½ (15-ounce) cans sweetened condensed milk

4 large egg yolks

1 cup freshly squeezed lime juice

Zest from 2 to 3 limes, about 2 teaspoons

Fresh whipped cream for garnish

Preheat the oven to 350 degrees F.

In a medium bowl, mix the graham cracker crumbs, melted butter, sugar, and salt until it resembles wet sand. Press crumbs into a 9x13-inch baking dish. Bake 10 minutes, then remove from oven to cool on a wire rack.

In a large bowl, whisk together the sweetened condensed milk, egg yolks, juice, and zest. Continue whisking until all ingredients are combined well and mixture has begun to thicken. Pour into the cooled crust, return to the oven, and bake 15 minutes.

Cool on a wire rack and then refrigerate 3 to 4 hours, or until set. Serve with fresh whipped cream.

Serves 9 to 12.

PEACHES-AND-CREAM BARS

Peaches are one of our favorite ingredients to cook with. Big, fuzzy orange globes dripping with sweet nectar—delicious! We pile them into a sweet bar complete with creamy filling and a brown-sugar butter streusel that is good enough to eat alone. (But it's better with the peaches.)

3 peaches, peeled and sliced

4 ounces cream cheese, softened

⅓ cup powdered sugar

1 egg, beaten

½ teaspoon vanilla

½ teaspoon salt

1 cup all-purpose flour

1 cup quick oats

1 teaspoon baking soda

¾ cup (1½ sticks) unsalted butter, melted and cooled

¾ cup brown sugar

Preheat oven to 350 degrees F. Coat an 8x8-inch baking dish with non-stick cooking spray.

In a medium bowl, with an electric hand mixer, combine the cream cheese, powdered sugar, egg, and vanilla until smooth. Set aside.

In a separate bowl, whisk together salt and flour. Add the oats, baking soda, melted butter, and brown sugar. Stir with a wooden spoon until everything is moist.

Press half of the oats mixture into the baking dish and bake 8 minutes. Remove from the oven and allow to cool 10 to 15 minutes.

Spread the cream cheese mixture over the bottom and layer with sliced peaches.

Sprinkle the remaining crumble mixture over the top and bake an additional 15 minutes. Cool, then chill in refrigerator until ready to serve.

Serves 6 to 9.

FUDGE BROWNIE COOKIES

So which is it? Brownies or cookies? Cade can never decide if he wants hot brownies and ice cream or crisp-on-the-edges-and-gooey-in-the-middle cookies, so we just compromise: brownie cookies! It's like a brownie, but in cookie form. Hello, deliciousness!

8 ounces unsweetened chocolate, chopped

8 ounces Baker's German Chocolate, chopped

¼ cup (½ stick) unsalted butter, at room temperature

4 eggs

1⅓ cups granulated sugar

1 teaspoon vanilla extract

½ cup plus 1 tablespoon all-purpose flour

¼ teaspoon salt

½ teaspoon baking powder

1¼ cups milk chocolate chips

Preheat oven to 350 degrees F. Line two cookie sheets with parchment paper to help reduce sticking, and set aside.

Place chocolate and butter in a glass bowl and set it over a saucepan of barely simmering water, stirring occasionally, until completely melted, shiny, and smooth.

Meanwhile, stir together eggs, sugar, and vanilla in a medium bowl and set aside.

In a small bowl, sift together flour, salt, and baking powder.

Add a little of the melted chocolate to the egg mixture, stirring continually to warm the mixture slightly and avoid curdling the eggs. Add the rest of the melted chocolate mixture to the egg mixture and stir to combine well. Slowly add the dry ingredients, folding them into the batter with a rubber spatula.

Once all of the flour is incorporated, stir in the chocolate chips.

Scoop 1½ tablespoons of dough onto baking sheets. Bake 10 to 12 minutes or until cookies are set. Do not overbake! Remove from oven and let cookies cool completely on the baking sheets.

Makes 2 dozen cookies.

CARAMEL BROWNIES

Carrian writes, "These are Mom's famous brownies I grew up with—even choosing them instead of cake for my birthday. This version is made from scratch instead of using a boxed mix. These brownies are also what caused our first disagreement when we were dating. I surprised Cade—a self-professed health nut—with these brownies on his birthday. He didn't eat them! I was so bummed. Eventually, he tried them (even though he wasn't eating sugar at the time) and they instantly became his guilty pleasure. Men should always listen to women, right, ladies?"

1 (11-ounce) package caramel squares, unwrapped

2/3 cup plus 2 tablespoons evaporated milk, divided

1½ cups flour

2 cups sugar

½ cup plus 1 tablespoon Dutch processed cocoa powder

1½ teaspoons baking powder

1½ teaspoons baking soda

1 teaspoon salt

¾ cup plus 1 tablespoon unsalted butter, melted

1¼ cup chocolate chips

Preheat oven to 350 degrees F. and grease a 9x13-inch baking pan.

Place caramels and ⅓ cup of the evaporated milk in a microwave-safe dish. Heat at high power in 30-second intervals, stirring in between each, until smooth and melted.

In another large bowl, whisk together the flour, sugar, cocoa, baking powder, baking soda, and salt.

Add the melted butter and remaining ⅓ cup plus 2 tablespoons evaporated milk and stir with a wooden spoon until the batter is thick, with no floury streaks remaining.

Spread and press half of the batter into the prepared pan. Bake 8 minutes, remove from the oven, and sprinkle evenly with chocolate chips. Slowly pour the melted caramel evenly over the entire surface of the brownies to be sure that everything is covered in caramel.

Using your hands, scoop up palm-sized portions of the remaining brownie batter and press flat between your hands. Gently lay over the caramel until covered. Return to oven and bake 15 minutes.

Cool before cutting into bars.

Serves 9 to 12.

CRANBERRY TOFFEE OATMEAL CHIPPERS

Carrian writes, "These may look like nothing more than oatmeal raisin cookies with a twist, but they are so much more than that to me. My very first baking memory is of making oatmeal cookies with my dad. I remember sitting on the counter, watching the mixer whir, and sampling the dough. I couldn't have been more than 3 years old. It was the beginning of my cooking journey. These cookies are an adaptation of those I used to make with Dad. They taste delicious and will always remind me of the importance of cooking with our children."

¾ cup Craisins

¼ cup (½ stick) unsalted butter, softened

¼ cup shortening

¼ cup granulated sugar

½ cup brown sugar

1 large egg, whisked

2 teaspoons vanilla

¾ cup all-purpose flour

1½ cups old fashioned oats

½ teaspoon ground cinnamon

⅛ teaspoon salt

2 teaspoons baking soda

1¼ cups semisweet chocolate chips

¾ cup Heath Milk Chocolate Toffee Bits

Place the Craisins in a small saucepan and add just enough water to cover the Craisins. Over medium heat, bring the water and Craisins just to a boil. As soon as Craisins have plumped, drain off the water, transfer to a bowl, and cool in the refrigerator.

In the bowl of an electric stand mixer, beat the butter and shortening until smooth, about 1 minute. Scrape down the sides of the bowl and add the sugars. Starting at low speed and gradually increasing to medium speed, beat 1 to 2 minutes, until light and fluffy.

Scrape down the sides of the bowl again and add the egg and vanilla. Mix until well incorporated, about 30 seconds.

In a small bowl, gently stir together the flour, oats, cinnamon, salt, and baking soda. Add to the wet ingredients and mix for 30 seconds.

Remove Craisins from refrigerator and blot dry with paper towels. Scrape down the sides of the bowl and add the Craisins, chocolate chips, and toffee, mixing until just combined. Scrape the sides down one last time and tightly cover the bowl with plastic wrap. Chill in the refrigerator 1 to 2 hours.

Preheat oven to 350 degrees F. Line a baking sheet with parchment paper. Scoop out rounded tablespoons of the dough onto the baking sheet and bake for 8 to 9 minutes. Remove the cookies from the oven when they still look slightly underbaked but have begun crisping around the edges. Cool on baking sheet for 2 minutes, then remove to a cooling rack.

Makes 2 to 3 dozen cookies.

PEANUT-BUTTER CINNAMON MELTAWAY COOKIES

Peanut butter is king at our house; we all love it. Our peanut butter cookies are soft and squishy, secretly stuffed with chocolate and then rolled in cinnamon sugar. Could they be the best peanut butter cookie out there? Taste for yourself.

½ cup (1 stick) unsalted butter, softened

½ cup granulated sugar

½ cup brown sugar

½ cup creamy peanut butter

1 large egg

½ teaspoon vanilla

½ teaspoon baking soda

½ teaspoon baking powder

½ teaspoon salt

1¼ cups all-purpose flour

⅓ cup cinnamon sugar for rolling

1½ cups milk chocolate baking discs or chocolate chunks

Preheat oven to 350 degrees F. Line baking sheets with parchment paper.

In the bowl of an electric stand mixer, combine butter and sugars, mixing on medium-high speed 1 to 2 minutes, until the mixture becomes creamy. Add peanut butter and mix until smooth.

Add the egg and vanilla, and mix to combine, about 30 seconds.

In a separate bowl, whisk together baking soda, baking powder, salt, and flour. Slowly add dry ingredients to the wet ingredients with the mixer running on low. Mix until combined and then turn off the mixer.

Place cinnamon sugar in a shallow bowl. Scoop a tablespoon of the dough into your hand and flatten it out on your palm. Place a Meltaway on top, fold the dough over the chocolate, and then roll into a ball. Roll the dough ball in the cinnamon sugar and place on prepared baking sheet.

Bake 8 to 10 minutes and remove from the oven. Serve warm.

Makes 2 dozen cookies.

MILLION DOLLAR COOKIE PIE

Cade is a die-hard cookie fan, and Carrian loves a fat slice of pie, so this cookie pie is the perfect solution. And to make it even more amazing, we added Dulce de Leche and chocolate hazelnut spread to the bottom, which then oozes out on the plate. This is the stuff dreams are made of!

½ cup butter, softened

½ cup granulated sugar

¼ cup packed light brown sugar

1 large egg

1¼ teaspoons vanilla

1½ cups all-purpose flour

½ teaspoon salt

½ teaspoon baking soda

½ cup semisweet chocolate chips

¼ cup milk chocolate chips

Pastry for a single-crust pie

¾ cup chocolate hazelnut spread

¾ cup Dulce de Leche

Sea salt flakes

Ice cream

Hot fudge sauce

Caramel sauce

Place the pie plate you will use for baking on top of a piece of parchment paper and use a pencil to trace the outline of the bottom of the plate. Set the parchment paper aside.

In a stand mixer with the paddle attachment in place, cream together the butter and sugars at medium speed for 2 minutes. Add the egg and vanilla and mix an additional minute.

In a separate bowl, whisk together the flour, salt, and baking soda. Add to wet ingredients and mix to combine.

Stir in chocolate chips and set aside.

Roll out pastry dough and line your pie plate. Trim and flute edges as desired. Cover with plastic wrap and refrigerate.

Take the parchment paper on which you traced an outline of the pie plate and place it, traced-side down, on the counter. You will be able to see the outline through the paper, but the pencil markings will be touching the counter, not the topping.

Scoop the hazelnut spread into the center of the parchment circle and spread out evenly to fill in the entire shape. Freeze 10 minutes, remove from freezer, spread Dulce de Leche over the top, and return to the freezer another 10 minutes.

Preheat oven to 350 degrees F.

Remove frozen hazelnut and Dulce de Leche disc from the freezer and carefully peel it off the parchment paper. Lay the disc in the pie crust. Add the cookie dough and gently press in about halfway up, reserving any remaining dough (if there is any) for cookies.

Bake for 20 to 30 minutes or until the top is golden brown and the center is almost set.

Remove from the oven and sprinkle with sea salt flakes. Allow to cool for about 30 minutes and then slice and serve with ice cream and toppings.

Serves 6 to 8.

PUMPKIN CUPCAKES WITH 7-MINUTE MAPLE FROSTING

Carrian writes, "When I was born, the nurses gave me the nickname 'Care Bear.' When I was a little girl, my mom made this 7-minute frosting for my Care Bear cake, and I've loved it ever since. When I went to frost these tender pumpkin cupcakes, I knew I had to bring back a classic flavor in a new way."

½ cup canola oil

¼ cup (½ stick) unsalted butter, softened

1¼ cups granulated sugar

3 large eggs

3 cups all-purpose flour

3 teaspoons pumpkin pie spice

2 teaspoons baking powder

1 teaspoon baking soda

¾ teaspoon nutmeg

½ teaspoon salt

¾ cup buttermilk

1 (15-ounce) can pumpkin

1 teaspoon vanilla

7-Minute Maple Frosting

Preheat oven to 350 degrees F. and line muffin tins with paper cups.

In a large bowl with an electric mixer, beat oil, butter, and sugar until smooth. Add eggs one at a time and beat on low until fluffy.

In a separate bowl, whisk together flour, pumpkin pie spice, baking powder, baking soda, nutmeg, and salt.

Add ⅓ of the dry ingredients to the wet mixture and beat just until combined. Add ½ of the buttermilk, beat to combine, and follow up with another ⅓ of the dry ingredients, the remaining buttermilk, and finally the rest of the dry ingredients, mixing to combine after each addition.

Stir in the pumpkin and vanilla by hand.

Spoon batter into lined muffin cups ¾ full and bake 20 to 22 minutes.

Frost cooled cupcakes while frosting is still hot.

Makes 24 to 36 cupcakes.

7-MINUTE MAPLE FROSTING

¾ cup Grade B pure maple syrup

1¼ cups granulated sugar

2 egg whites

¼ teaspoon cream of tartar

Pinch salt

Combine all ingredients in the top of a double boiler and beat with an electric hand mixer for 1 minute.

Place pan over simmering water, being careful not to let water touch the bottom of the pan.

Beat with an electric mixer 7 minutes, until stiff peaks have formed.

Remove from heat and use immediately.

CHOCOLATE BANANA CAKE WITH CHOCOLATE CREAM-CHEESE FROSTING

Every Southerner has a classic banana cream-cheese bar recipe, but what about a chocolate-on-chocolate banana snack cake? Top this super-moist cake with a smooth, rich chocolate cream-cheese frosting and your friends and family will be begging to live with you. Oh, in that case, maybe you better not even open that door . . .

¼ cup (½ stick) butter, softened

½ cup brown sugar

¼ cup granulated sugar

½ teaspoon vanilla

2 large eggs, slightly beaten

1 cup all-purpose flour

½ cup cocoa powder

½ teaspoon baking soda

½ teaspoon salt

1 cup mashed ripe bananas (about 2 small bananas)

Chocolate Cream-Cheese Frosting

Preheat oven to 350 degrees F. Coat a 9x9-inch baking dish with non-stick cooking spray.

To the bowl of an electric stand mixer, add butter, sugars, vanilla, and eggs and beat until smooth and creamy, 2 to 3 minutes.

In a separate bowl, whisk together the flour, cocoa, baking soda, and salt until combined well.

Add ⅓ of the dry ingredients to the butter mixture and mix briefly. Add half of the mashed banana and mix again. Add ⅓ of the dry ingredients, mix briefly, and then add the rest of the banana. Mix again, add the remaining dry ingredients, and mix one last time, scraping down the sides of the bowl as needed. Do not overmix.

Spread batter in prepared pan and bake 20 to 30 minutes, until a toothpick inserted 1 inch from the edge of the pan comes out clean.

Allow cake to cool until it is still slightly room temperature and then frost generously and gently with Chocolate Cream-Cheese Frosting.

Serves 6 to 9.

CHOCOLATE CREAM-CHEESE FROSTING

2 ounces cream cheese, softened

¼ cup (½ stick) butter, softened

2 tablespoons heavy cream

1 tablespoon cocoa powder

2 cups powdered sugar

With an electric mixer, beat cream cheese, butter, heavy cream, cocoa, and powdered sugar until smooth.

OLD-FASHIONED SPUDNUT DONUTS

You haven't really had donuts until you've had these fluffy guys. Yes, they're made with potatoes, but they're so light and airy, they're perfectly heavenly. Serve with hot cocoa or cider, and they will be gone in no time.

2 to 3 medium Yukon gold potatoes

2 large eggs, beaten slightly

1 cup whole milk

1 cup granulated sugar

5 teaspoons baking powder

1 teaspoon salt

3 tablespoons shortening or lard, melted

2 teaspoons vanilla

3 to 4 cups all-purpose flour

Canola or peanut oil

¾ cup cinnamon sugar for dredging, placed in a shallow bowl

Bring a saucepan of water to boil over high heat and add the potatoes with the peels still on. Cook 15 to 20 minutes, until tender. Let potatoes cool slightly and then mash in a large bowl with skins on until no chunks remain. Measure mashed potatoes. Keep 1 cup in the bowl and discard any extra.

Add the eggs and milk to the potatoes and stir well to combine.

In a separate, smaller bowl, whisk together sugar and baking powder to combine. Stir into the potato mixture, followed by the salt, shortening, and vanilla.

Add the flour, 1 cup at a time, until a soft, slightly sticky dough forms. You may not need the full 4 cups flour. Do not knead the dough.

Heat 4 to 5 inches of oil in a cast-iron pot to medium-high, or 375 degrees F.

While oil heats, roll out dough on a floured surface about ½-inch thick. Cut out donuts with a donut cutter and carefully add a few at a time to the hot oil. To prevent oil from splashing and burning you, do not drop the donuts in the oil from more than 1 or 2 inches above the oil. Turn donuts constantly with a metal spider strainer or slotted spoon until golden brown. Drain off excess oil on a paper-towel lined plate and then immediately dredge hot donuts in cinnamon sugar.

Serves 8 to 10.

CHOCOLATE-STRAWBERRY GRILLED CROISSANTS

Grilled croissants make the perfect canvas for silky chocolate hazelnut spread and sweet berries. Their flaky layers are light and buttery, and the chocolate and fresh berries piled inside combine for a totally Southern and Pacific Northwest flavor explosion.

4 croissants, sliced open

Butter, softened

Chocolate hazelnut spread (like Nutella)

Sliced strawberries

Freshly whipped, sweetened cream

Spread a very light coat of butter over each croissant half.

On a grill pan or outdoor grill heated to medium heat, place the croissant halves facedown and grill just until marks appear, 1 to 2 minutes.

Quickly apply a generous layer of chocolate hazelnut spread over half of the grilled croissants, top with berries and whipped cream, followed by the croissant tops. Serve with a dollop of whipped cream on top.

Serves 4.

CHURRO-STYLE BREAD PUDDING

Bread pudding is a familiar and favorite recipe and one we can totally get behind. There's nothing very pudding-y about it because the custard is absorbed by all that flaky croissant goodness. Serve it up with extra Dulce de Leche or caramel sauce and you've got Churro-Style Bread Pudding!

1 (15-ounce) can Dulce de Leche

5 to 6 croissants, torn into pieces

1 cup half-and-half

1 cup heavy cream

4 large eggs

1 teaspoon vanilla

½ teaspoon ground cinnamon

Fresh whipped cream for garnishing

Cinnamon sugar for garnishing

Coat an 8x8-inch baking dish with nonstick cooking spray. Pour half the Dulce de Leche over the bottom of the pan and scatter with torn croissant pieces.

In a large bowl, whisk together the half-and-half, cream, eggs, vanilla, and cinnamon. Pour over the top of the bread and refrigerate 1 hour, pressing the bread down into the liquid after 30 minutes.

Preheat an oven to 350 degrees F. Place the pan of soaked croissants in a large roasting pan and fill with water halfway up the smaller pan. Carefully transfer to oven and bake 1 hour and 25 minutes until set.

Remove from the oven and allow to cool 5 to 10 minutes.

To serve, scoop into individual bowls and top with additional Dulce de Leche, fresh whipped cream, and a sprinkling of cinnamon sugar.

Serves 6 to 10.

LEMON CHEESECAKE MOUSSE CUPS

We grew up loving cheesecake mousse cups. But the recipe of our youth called for nondairy whipped topping and canned pie filling. We think it's time for an update using homemade lemon curd. It's light, bright, and pretty much the best thing we've ever eaten. In fact, we always stand around the empty pot and dip strawberries in the leftover curd. So yummy!

2 cups heavy cream, divided

2 cups powdered sugar, divided

3 (8-ounce) packages cream cheese, softened

2 cups Lemon Curd (see recipe below)

1 teaspoon lemon zest

4 tablespoons water

2 tablespoons freshly squeezed lemon juice

2 tablespoons unflavored gelatin

½ teaspoon yellow food coloring (optional)

Fresh blackberries, strawberries, blueberries, and raspberries for serving

½ lemon, sliced and quartered for garnishing

In a medium bowl with an electric mixer, beat the heavy cream into stiff peaks. Add ¼ cup of the powdered sugar and beat again to incorporate; set aside.

In a large bowl, using a handheld mixer, beat the cream cheese until smooth, about 2 to 3 minutes. Add in the lemon zest, lemon curd, and ¾ cup of the powdered sugar; beat again until smooth and set aside.

In a small, microwave-safe bowl, stir together the water and lemon juice and sprinkle the gelatin over the top. Let sit for 1 minute.

Heat gelatin mixture in the microwave on high power for 25 seconds. Let it rest 2 to 3 minutes and then beat it into cream cheese mixture.

Fold in half of the whipped cream until combined well. Spoon (or add mousse to a pastry bag and pipe it) into serving dishes. Chill in refrigerator 2 hours, up to overnight, reserving leftover whipped cream in the fridge until ready to serve.

For serving, pile the top of each dish with fruit, give the whipped cream a good whisking again and add a dollop to each dish. Garnish with lemon wedges and serve immediately.

Serves 4.

LEMON CURD

6 large eggs

8 large egg yolks

2 teaspoons lemon zest

1½ cups fresh lemon juice (about 6 to 8 large lemons)

1½ cups granulated sugar

Pinch salt

10 tablespoons unsalted butter, chopped

In a large bowl, beat the eggs and egg yolks together until pale in color, about 1 minute; set aside.

In a heavy pot over medium heat, combine the lemon zest, juice, sugar, and salt. Cook, stirring, until the sugar has dissolved, about 5 minutes.

Remove from heat and whisk a few tablespoons of the hot lemon mixture into the beaten eggs to temper them.

Stir the tempered eggs into the hot lemon and return saucepan to burner. Cook over medium heat 5 to 8 minutes, or until the mixture coats the back of a spoon and is thickened.

Remove from heat and press through a mesh strainer over a clean bowl to remove any tiny pieces of cooked egg.

Quickly stir in the butter until melted and combined.

Fill a container or bowl with the curd and press plastic wrap tightly against the top (this prevents a skin from forming on top). Refrigerate until cool. Store in an airtight container with plastic wrap up to 2 weeks.

COOKIES AND CREAM FROZEN CUSTARD

Ice cream. Cade loves it. Carrian—not so much. Not until we had the creamiest, dreamiest frozen custard, and we've both been obsessed ever since. This classic take on cookies-and-cream is easy to make and since you can use a variety of cookies, it's a fun recipe to twist each time you make it.

2 cups heavy cream

1 cup half-and-half

1¼ cups granulated sugar

1 vanilla bean, seeds scraped out and reserved

6 egg yolks

1½ sleeves Oreo cookies, coarsely chopped or crumbled

In a large saucepan over medium-low heat, combine the cream, half-and-half, sugar, and the vanilla bean pod and seeds. Stir occasionally, heating the mixture until bubbles form around the edges. Remove from heat.

Meanwhile, in a medium bowl, vigorously whisk 6 egg yolks together until thick, frothy, and pale yellow in color. After removing the cream mixture from the heat, spoon 5 tablespoons of the hot cream, 1 tablespoon at a time, into the eggs while whisking continuously. This tempers the eggs so they do not begin to scramble when added to the hot cream. Return the saucepan of hot cream to the burner, set heat to medium-low, and slowly whisk in the tempered eggs, stirring constantly.

Heat, stirring continuously, until thickened. You should be able to dip a spoon into the mixture and have the cream coat the back of the spoon. To test, drag your finger through the cream on the back of the spoon; if it leaves a trail, you're done. Don't allow cream to get hotter than 160 degrees F.

Remove from heat, cool slightly, and then chill in the refrigerator covered in plastic wrap for several hours or overnight.

Once the mixture is chilled, remove the bean pod, and freeze according to the manufacturer's directions for your 4- to 5-quart ice cream maker.

When ice cream is almost done churning, add ⅔ of the crushed Oreo cookies to the ice cream and let machine finish churning. Transfer ice cream to a freezer-safe container a few scoops at a time, adding some of the remaining cookie pieces after every few scoops. Freeze at least 4 hours before serving.

Serves 4 to 6.

index

Page numbers in *italics* refer to images.